STuP
SMOKING
THE EASY WAY

STOP
SMOKING
THE EASY WAY

5

simple steps
to freedom

Sue Wells

NEW
HOLLAND

First published in 2007 by New Holland Publishers (UK) Ltd
London • Cape Town • Sydney • Auckland
www.newhollandpublishers.com

10 9 8 7 6 5 4 3 2 1

Garfield House, 86–88 Edgware Road, London W2 2EA, UK
80 McKenzie Street, Cape Town 8001, South Africa
14 Aquatic Drive, Frenchs Forest, NSW 2086, Australia
218 Lake Road, Northcote, Auckland, New Zealand

Copyright © 2007 in text: Sue Wells
Copyright © 2007 New Holland Publishers (UK) Ltd

All rights reserved. No part of this publication may be reproduced, stored in a retrieval
system or transmitted, in any form or by any means, electronic, mechanical, photocopy-
ing, recording or otherwise, without the prior written permission of the publishers and
copyright holders.

ISBN 978 184537 535 5

Editorial Director: Jo Hemmings
Project Editor: Kate Parker
Editor: Liz O'Donnell
Design and cover design: Adam Morris
Production: Hema Gohil

Reproduction by Pica Digital PTE Ltd, Singapore.
Printed and bound in India by Replika Press Pvt. Ltd.

Publisher's Note: The author and publishers have made every effort to ensure that the
information contained in this book is correct at the time of going to press, and they
accept no responsibility for any loss, injury or inconvenience sustained by any person
through using this book.

Acknowledgements

Thanks to all my friends who have encouraged and supported me, especially
Angie Sage, Hamish Hodgen, Sara Francis, Miriam Akhtar, Sabine Wells,
Amanda Ashby, Vaughn Malcom, daughters Catherine, Anna and Sophie,
the late, lovely Lorna Flinton and to all the smokers and quitters I've worked
with, including those at Pembroke Road Surgery, Bristol and Southmead
Support to Stop, Avon; and to all my clients in the UK and abroad, from
whom I have learnt so much. To Jo Hemmings at New Holland for taking
me on so spontaneously, and to my editor Kate Parker for her enthusiasm,
respect and wonderfully impressive warmth and efficiency. Also, to all those
who have contributed to the richness of the book via their quotations.

To Ken and Elizabeth Mellor, whose inspirational teaching over many years has helped me write this book and whose materials I have adapted in the hope that I, in turn, can inspire others – most particularly, smokers to quit. In recognition of their work, the first ten per cent of my profits from the book will be tithed with much gratitude to the Biame Network.

And to Martin, my husband, for his love, support and endless editing on long car journeys.

CONTENTS

PART 3: ACTION:
THE FIVE SESSION PROGRAMME

Introduction: Setting out

'When the student is ready the teacher appears', Buddha

Do you want to transform your life? To enjoy it more fully, to feel really good about yourself, free from worries about your health and weight, to save money? Do you want to be able to relax, concentrate and cope in a crisis? Imagine doing all this relatively easily, without the aid of cigarettes. Or having to rely on willpower.

Sounds too good to be true? Most smokers would like to quit – at least 70 per cent. Like them, you probably have good intentions, especially around New Year and National No Smoking Day, but somehow it never happens. Or you've tried lots of different methods, but don't manage to stay stopped for long.

How is it that some smokers manage to stop smoking easily while others struggle, get stuck or start smoking again within a short time? When you haven't succeeded in the past, do you feel a failure, criticize yourself and resume smoking? Do you then hold onto this experience of failure as a reason for not making any further quit attempts, or do you allow it to sabotage future attempts?

'Just as we learn how to start and not finish, we can learn to complete what we begin', SARK, _Juicy Living Cards_ (Hay House, 2003)

We learn through repetition

What if you could turn this around so, instead, you see past attempts as a measure of how serious you are about wanting to stop smoking and so you understand that we learn through repetition? It may be that you haven't yet completed the learning process, which might be why it feels like you keep returning (yourself) to 'the beginning' again.

'Over and over we have to go back to the beginning. We should not be ashamed of this. It is good. It is like drinking water', Natalie Goldberg, _Writing Down the Bones_ (Shambala Publications, 1986)

By using this book, you can complete this learning, free yourself from the misery of relapse and enjoy your life much more fully without cigarettes and the permanent shadow of threatened ill health.

'Suspend judgment and see where your exploration takes you', Michael Harner, *The Way of the Shaman* (Harper Collins, 1990)

Open your mind

What this book will teach you may be unlike anything you have learnt before. It requires you to open your mind to the possibility of stopping smoking, to suspend your judgement and to allow yourself to experiment with new ways of learning. These ways include drawing on your own natural powers and resources to help you attain your goal and teach you how to have faith in your own ability to deal successfully with the challenges of stopping smoking for good.

Empower yourself

The book is not about scaring you, bullying you or frightening you. It's the complete opposite; it's empowering and optimistic. I want it to excite, inspire and challenge you! Lots of smokers feel that the challenges are too great. 'If only' you had a magic wand; 'if only' you'd never started smoking. You probably feel appalled when you see children smoking, especially if they're your own, knowing that this could mean a potentially fatal or damaging lifelong addiction.

Many of you would like to be free from smoking, but say you enjoy cigarettes too much – or else you've tried and 'can't' stop. Others keep putting it off because you say there's never a good time to do it – you're starting a new job, going on holiday, too busy or too stressed at work. You get overwhelmed by the idea of stopping smoking and tell yourself it's too difficult, then convince yourself there's no real need at the moment, ignoring the risks to your health and imagining you're safe from an addiction that is now estimated to kill around half of all smokers.

So, congratulations – the fact that you're looking at this book means you've taken the first step in a journey that could transform and lengthen your life. At last, here is an opportunity to change direction and start new ways of seeing and doing things. Once you begin this process, you may find you're no longer able to continue behaving in the same way as you did before.

Turning points

This is your way of helping yourself move on, of taking that first step. However tiny, however reluctant it may be, it is helping to change the way you think about yourself and about smoking and what it does for you. It is the first step in encouraging yourself to look at how smoking affects your health, self-esteem, well being, relationships, finances – and how you may have let smoking dictate the way you live your life.

The act of reviewing your decision to smoke could be your turning point, your moment of realization. It can happen in a split second – like falling in love – like the flick of a switch. But turning points can also be gradual and evolve. They may take time, so there's no need to pressurize yourself. It can be helpful to take little steps, to make little changes; these can lead to big changes. In fact, little and often is a fundamental recipe for success.

Turning points can sometimes be triggered by 'outer signals' such as a health scare – either your own or someone you know who smokes. Or they could be triggered by 'inner signals': you're turning 30 or 40 or 50; you're getting married; you want to have a baby. Or you realize that smoking has outlived its 'usefulness'. It's now just a habit and no longer fits with the way you want to live your life.

Whatever form it takes, the same situation applies: something that was true for you for maybe years ('I don't want to stop', 'I can't stop' or 'I enjoy it too much') is beginning to be true no longer. Maybe it's just a thought or a feeling at the moment. But from this point on, life can be very different for you!

SELF-COACHING TIPS

• *Take time out to reflect: 'What changes could make my life more satisfying?' Make a note of these:*

_____

_____

_____

> • If you want to make a change in your life – no matter how small a step to start with – you need to make that change a part of your everyday life.
> • Embracing change in this way will help you realize your goal more easily. You do this by staying in touch with the desire for change, which has already been stirred up in you, and beginning to think and feel differently about yourself in relation to smoking. This step can be as slow or fast as you want; for example, think about why you're lighting up; what need is it fulfilling in you?

Quick preview

'Change is a journey. Take a guide', Sheppard Moscow Personal Development manual

The book is divided into three parts:

PART 1 introduces you to the possibility of change and focuses mostly on the psychological aspects of smoking: what keeps you hooked in? What does smoking do for you (and to you)? What changes might help you?

PART 2 is your 'toolkit for success'. You'll find the techniques in this section will help you focus on what you need to do to make these changes work for you. This 'toolkit' of five techniques, or steps, enables you to respond to different situations in different ways, for example, by staying calm, by dealing with self-sabotage or by helping keep you on track.

PART 3 includes a progressive five-session programme that has helped many quitters to stop smoking successfully and to avoid – or successfully manage – relapse.

Familiarizing yourself with Parts 1 and 2 means that the sessions that follow will complement what you've learnt.
Most chapters contain:
• a personal self-awareness quiz and various exercises that you can complete by writing in the spaces provided;
• self-coaching tips and information, strategies and fact boxes;
• a self-assessment scale to measure and affirm your commitment as we go along and alert you to particular areas you may need to attend to.

Each chapter can be followed in sequence or you can revisit them until you feel ready to move on. This point is important as it often mirrors the experience of quitters who need to keep repeating certain aspects around changing their behaviour before they feel ready to make that change permanent. How many times have you ('knowingly') put yourself in a vulnerable position by going to the pub before you're 'ready'?

Go at your own pace

What's important is to keep things going at a pace that suits you. Celebrate each step, no matter how small, as you go along. Notice these small steps even if they seem tiny, like thoughts about quitting or just 'observing' yourself smoking. See them as progress. Reward yourself.

Understanding your addiction and learning new and different ways of dealing with your desire to smoke can take time. So respect your resistance. You've probably been smoking for a long time and any major change will require some adjustments.

The sessions are there for you to use and build on. Repeat sessions as many times as you like in order to learn each step as fully as you feel you need, before moving onto the next one. You may need to spend more time on some sessions than others, depending on your own personal needs.

All the sessions support and connect with one another, and you'll become increasingly familiar with the process as you move on. This familiarity will also be your main clue as to your readiness to move on.

The book is interactive, which means that through the exercises and quizzes, you'll be actively involved in the process of learning what you need to do to make the necessary changes to your life.

Keep it with you and – very importantly – keep it private and keep it safe. It's your own personal record of your thoughts, feelings and actions about your smoking so it's important to feel you can record what you want to, to allow a 'free flow' rather than editing it for fear of censure. See it as your friend, your 'confidante'.

Setting your own quit date

Part 3 involves setting your quit date, when you feel ready to do so. By this time you'll have understood your addiction and how it affects you. You'll have learnt to take the seduction and power out of smoking.

You'll be expecting to succeed, having resolved any inner conflicts about quitting. And you'll be looking forward to finishing with cigarettes. And staying that way.

How are you feeling?

How do you feel right now? Comfortable, excited, fascinated, slightly fearful or plain terrified? Whatever you're feeling right now will give you some clues as to just that: how you're feeling at the moment. This is a really useful phrase because what you're experiencing will change with your mastery of the techniques as you go along. So enjoy the process. Carry this guide with you, maybe use it on the train, the bus or whenever you have a few minutes to yourself. Commit to using it every day. Whether or not you're thinking seriously about quitting at the moment, if you're unable or unwilling to take that first step – this will help you move on. So let's get going!

PART 1: MOTIVATION

1 How to set out

'It is only when the mind is open and receptive that learning and seeing and change can occur', Jon Kabat-Zinn, *Full Catastrophe Living* (Piatkus, 2001)

Whatever prompted you to pick up this book, it can support, encourage, challenge and inspire you to take action to stop smoking.

The techniques you're about to learn may be different to any you have come across before. This means you'll need to keep an open mind and be prepared to experiment with new ways of thinking and learning – proven ways that you can apply to improve other areas of your life as well. You'll find that accomplishing the tasks and exercises will help you establish your own momentum for change – the more you persevere, the greater your enjoyment and reward. You may experience immediate benefits from the techniques you learn, or it may take time to master them.

Take responsibility for your own actions

'We all experience our power in some ways and inhibit it by discounting it or pushing it onto someone else, thereby diminishing it', Elizabeth Mellor, educator and therapist

Taking responsibility for yourself – for your own actions – will enable you to manage yourself in a completely different way as regards your smoking. You can begin to take back control and – by focusing on 'taking it back' – you can empower yourself. The commitment you decide to make to take action is up to you.

'Money back' schemes for quitters and therapies that claim to 'cure' you of smoking shift the responsibility of creating your own success (or failure) away from you and onto someone else. And, as a result, the 'success' tends not to last.

Keep the momentum going

It's important to keep up some momentum, no matter how small, so you don't get stuck in one place. For example, take cutting down the number of cigarettes you smoke a day: if your goal is to quit, then you'll need to move on at some point. Cutting down may help formulate more clearly your decision to quit, but at the same time you also need to keep sight of your goal by working gently towards it.

Working your way through the book may be a straightforward experience and give you a real sense of progress, enabling you to quit successfully or to get the support you need. But it's important to remember that returning to chapters or exercises is also progress. You may need to repeat a chapter or exercise many times before you feel you've mastered it as much as you need in order to move on.

Mastering the techniques is crucial. Why do you think at least 70 per cent of quitters return to smoking within a year of quitting? It's because they haven't mastered effective ways of dealing with the urge to smoke.

Feel confident with each step before you move on. Progress in your own time and in your own way. Be alert to your needs and do what feels right. Don't rush in the mistaken belief that this is the best way to succeed.

Become your own coach

You will learn how to become your own stop-smoking coach: how to be kind to yourself, like a mother to her vulnerable child; how to nurture and encourage yourself. People don't usually harm themselves deliberately, and that includes smokers. So take yourself out of the endless cycle of guilt and self-criticism, shame or self-destructiveness.

You will learn how to be firm with yourself in a loving way; how to set limits for yourself; how to forgive; how to avoid persecuting; how to be patient with yourself; how to respect what you're doing. You'll learn to respect any resistance, defences or ambivalence you may have, to find ways of dealing with your 'inner rebel'. This may include starting to believe that quitting smoking can seriously improve your health, wealth and looks.

'What progress, you ask, have I made? I have begun to be a friend to myself', Hecato, Roman philosopher

Like other new tasks in your life, you need to find out what works for you. Think of stopping smoking as a journey you're setting out on. It may be a straightforward direct trip, or it may have several 'stops'. It's up to you to decide for yourself how you get there. The journey may involve a complete change of lifestyle: physical, emotional and spiritual.

Knowledge is power

The only reasons that endure are the ones that arise from deep within us. Your situation is really about facing yourself. When you understand more about yourself and your addiction, you will be in a powerful position to make the necessary changes to protect yourself and to be involved in your complete recovery.

• What do you think will sustain you over the coming weeks?
• Will you continue to put your power 'outside' yourself?
• Will you do what you need to do – or decide the goal isn't worth it?
• Given what you know from your own experience, are you willing to forgo what you know is possible?

Associative memory

When you tell yourself that smoking is connected with pleasure and relaxation over and over, each time you light up, the pattern you set up in your brain actually changes your brain's structure. According to the recent science film, 'What The Bleep Do We Know?', the nerve cells and receptors 'wire together' and 'fire together'. This is called associative memory.

The good news is that every time we interrupt the relationship between the nerve cells – by interrupting the thought processes – it breaks the pattern. The way you do this is to change 'I can't enjoy life without a cigarette' into 'I can enjoy life' – an affirmation that will ultimately help you to stop smoking.

This applies to any repetitive behaviour or attitude to anything you want to change – including your view of the world. You're 'rewiring' your brain when you make different choices – so, ultimately, you change yourself from inside out.

Self-programming

Are you aware you programme yourself exactly according to your own inner thoughts and feelings – via messages you anchor in your brain? You set your own programme, even though you may not be conscious of it.

Be aware of what you say to yourself and others about your smoking or quitting and get into the habit of believing what you tell yourself. Like programming a computer, only the positive information gets anchored. Establish a good, honest relationship with yourself to help you quit as easily as possible.

One friend could have changed the course of her life if she'd known what it meant to 'anchor' ideas. She was a smoker who told herself when she was younger, 'I'd better give up before it kills me... when I'm old – about 45!' On the morning of her 45th birthday, she was going downstairs and suffered a massive heart attack. After years of fighting for her life, the trauma of a heart transplant, endless medication and hospital visits, she now has a completely different lifestyle.

The things we tell ourselves can have a strong impact on us. We internalize them as true, because our brain – like a computer – registers them as real or actual – it doesn't know you're exaggerating. Or making moral judgements.

The following words are common examples of the potential power of simple, often everyday, words. Be mindful of them.

- 'Always' means 'always' ('I always fail').
- 'Never' means 'never' ('I'll never do it').
- 'Difficult' means 'difficult' ('I know it'll be difficult').
- 'Easy' means 'easy' ('I expect it to be easy').

Who said it was easy?

You don't expect quitters these days to go 'cold turkey' (even the phrase is a deterrent) and say things like 'Stopping smoking was much easier than I thought'. It might even make you feel angry. 'Of course it's not easy.' For years you've been brainwashed with information that focuses on the exact opposite of 'easy' when it comes to quitting: 'It's hard, drives you mad, makes you fat – and you'll probably fail ... again.'

On top of this, you've been brainwashed into believing cigarettes enhance your image and way of life: you can't do certain things –

like relax or have a meal – without one. You believe this is true and therefore experience it as true. How will you possibly function without cigarettes?

Hypnotizing yourself

So you 'programme' yourself to expect a hard time, and that's exactly what happens. Your brain absorbs the message you've given it – that quitting is 'difficult'. You then hypnotize yourself into believing it's true – so you set yourself up to fail. (Maybe secretly you didn't really want to quit in the first place.) This failure, in turn, serves to confirm how hard it is to quit: you were right, you shouldn't have bothered and you'll never try again.

If language has the power to hypnotize you into believing quitting is hard, then use it to stimulate the belief that the opposite is true. See quitting as relatively easy. If people suggest you're bound to fail, use this negative comment to remind yourself of what you do want – that is, to succeed.

I remember one client dreading having to tell people – yet again – that she was quitting. She imagined their response, 'Oh, God, you're not stopping smoking again!' This time she had a different response ready: 'Yeah, and I'd really appreciate your support as a friend.'

Reframing means turning a negative comment into a positive one to help you achieve what you want – without offending anyone. It's also a good way to reaffirm or remind yourself what you want to achieve.

Quitters behave differently

Thinking and behaving in a different way can totally change the picture for you. It's a very freeing experience and can release you from being stuck with always having the same 'take' on things, like 'stopping smoking is really hard'. And you'll find other people respond to you differently as well. Experiment for yourself.

PREPARE YOUR REPLIES

What might people say when they hear you want to stop smoking?

1. _____
2. _____
3. _____

Now list three responses you might make that take on board what they're saying. Use their comments to 'reframe' them into a positive response by taking what they say and fine-tuning it so you hear what they say in a positive way, even if their message spells doom and gloom.

1. _____

2. _____

3. _____

Here are some examples:
'I suppose that means we can't go to the pub anymore' – 'We can go to the pub, but maybe not straight away.'
'Go on . . . keep me company, have a fag' – 'I'll keep you company, but I won't have a fag.'
'It took me loads of times to stop smoking and I still crave fags 20 years later' – 'Well, they say it can take a few times but I feel really good right now about wanting to stop smoking – and everyone's different.'

Create your own reality. Consciously choose a set of beliefs for yourself rather than allowing yourself to be brainwashed through advertising and the media or through your own language.

SELF-COACHING TIPS
You can influence what happens to you – including the real possibility of stopping smoking. You can pursue life without interference of addiction.

Commitment scale

How committed are you, at this point in time, to keep an open mind regarding the possibility of stopping smoking?
Rate yourself on a scale of 1 to 10, where 1 is no commitment and 10 is totally committed: 1 2 3 4 5 6 7 8 9 10

2 Getting under way

'The minute we are engaged in creating something, the something of our choice, we are back in our own power', Julia Cameron, *The Vein of Gold* (Pan, 1997)

You're in charge of your life and your actions. Whether you're aware of it or not, you have the power to create what you need for yourself at any moment. You can tap into this creativity – this ability to create what you want for yourself. Here you learn how.

HOW DO YOU FEEL ABOUT YOUR SMOKING?

The following questions will enable you to identify your attitude to smoking – your thoughts, feelings and actions about your habit. The questions below are only a rough guide to see where you are 'at the moment' so don't worry too much about them. You'll find your answers can change as you go along.

1 'Recently I've been asking myself "what's the point of smoking?" or "how come I'm still doing this?"'
• Yes
• Sometimes
• No

2. 'I feel confused about my smoking – part of me wants to stop but part of me doesn't.'
• Yes
• Sometimes
• No

3. 'It seems to get more difficult to make a decision about stopping smoking than it used to.'
• Yes
• Sometimes
• No

4. 'I can feel a bit uncomfortable and touchy around the subject of my smoking.'
• Yes
• Sometimes
• No

5. 'I can feel quite stirred up sometimes when I think about what I'm allowing smoking to do to me.'
• Yes
• Sometimes
• No

6. 'I sometimes wonder what's the worst thing that can happen if I were to stop smoking.'
• Yes
• Sometimes
• No

7. 'I am more open to thinking about stopping smoking than I used to be.'
• Yes
• Sometimes
• No

8. 'I realize smoking is not consistent with what I want in my life or what is important to me.'
• Yes
• Sometimes
• No

9. 'There are times when I can see myself managing without cigarettes.'
• Yes
• Sometimes
• No

10. 'There are times when this is how I'd like my life to be – free from smoking.'
• Yes
• Sometimes
• No

Now go back and circle the question or questions you feel apply most to you, then answer the following questions:

1. How do you feel about pressure from others to stop smoking?

_____

_____

_____

_____

2. If it affects you, even a tiny bit, do you think it's because part of you wants to stop smoking?
• Yes
• No
3. Do you ever listen to this part?
• Yes
• Sometimes
• No
4. You may not know why you're still smoking, but what do you think might help and encourage you to quit?

_____

_____

_____

_____

On a scale of 1 to 10 how important is it to you to quit?
1 2 3 4 5 6 7 8 9 10
On a scale of 1 to 10 how confident are you that you could quit?
1 2 3 4 5 6 7 8 9 10
What number between 1 and 10 would you need to score to be ready to think about quitting? 1 2 3 4 5 6 7 8 9 10
(Source: Martin Raw and Pip Mason, 'Motivation, the Ilkley Course')

The missing link
One crucial factor I remember from my own experience as a smoker, as well as many clients' experiences, which surfaces time and again, is the inability of quitters to stay quit. This may sound obvious but what happens is this: you decide you want to stop. You're fed up with smoking, with friends and family nagging, with feeling like a social leper, with smelling disgusting, with coughing and wheezing, with being unable to run for the bus, with being quietly plagued by fears of serious illness,

with being controlled by nicotine. So you go cold turkey, use self-help books, nicotine replacement therapy (NRT), have acupuncture, hypnotherapy, counselling, join a group, use a telephone counselling service. You may pay good money and are often really motivated to quit.

But there is one factor that is frequently overlooked by both quitters and health professionals alike. This is the need to resolve any inner conflicts or mixed feelings you may have about stopping smoking. This is a very real dilemma that many smokers face.

Ignoring your 'inner tug'

If you've tried to quit before or haven't been able to attempt it with confidence, you'll know it's vital not to underestimate the power of that 'deep down' part – the inner tug – where you're torn between the part of you that wants to stop and the part of you that doesn't.

Stumbling blocks

If you've tried to stop smoking before and failed, what do you think was the main reason? Alternatively, if you haven't tried quitting before, what do you think might be the main stumbling block for you?

_____

_____

_____

_____

Lots of smokers I've worked with say similar things when it comes to quitting, like 'I'm just not sure if, deep down, I really, really want to stop smoking'. We are reluctant to acknowledge this dilemma, and tend to repress, ignore or deny it.

Look at the expression 'giving up'. What does it mean? We assume it means wanting to kick the habit, but actually no one really wants to 'give up' anything. Yet this contradiction is very rarely dealt with in any depth.

It's assumed that if you want to stop smoking, the deep-down part of you that's not entirely sure is expected to simply dissolve or disappear. You may feel embarrassed acknowledging this dilemma. After all, if you want to achieve something in our culture, you focus on that goal; you shouldn't have mixed feelings about the very thing you want to leave behind – especially if it's something harmful.

Re-experiencing the pleasure of smoking

As part of your 'toolkit for success' (see Part 2), you will learn a unique and natural way to help release these intense feelings as part of the process of quitting. This technique even requires you to re-experience the pleasures of smoking – as much as you need.

Not surprisingly, this is not something that features on most professionals' agendas (or in other self-help books), but you'll find it's a very effective and proven way to help you resolve any deep-seated doubts.

One of the biggest steps towards final freedom from nicotine is understanding and dealing successfully with these doubts. Once they are resolved internally, they will automatically be resolved externally as well. It's really important and worth mentioning at this stage, as these doubts are almost always the main reason why quitters relapse.

EXPECTING TO SUCCEED PAYS OFF

Do you expect to succeed? Answer quickly and intuitively.

• Yes
• No
• Don't Know

The saying 'We tend to get what we expect' in life is a powerful one and can influence the outcome – either positively or negatively.

If Yes, how easy or difficult do you expect it to be?

_____

_____

_____

Do you want to succeed on the surface, but underneath, have doubts that may lead to self-sabotage?

• Yes
• No
• Don't Know

Are you secretly expecting to fail, like you've done in the past, because that's often been the pattern in your life?

• Yes
• No
• Don't Know

Stop smoking for good

You're capable of stopping smoking for good. You'll discover, as you work through the book, the secrets for long-term success are learning how to:

- focus on succeeding;
- understand your addiction and why you smoke;
- change the way you think about smoking and what it does for you;
- resolve any inner conflicts or doubts smoking creates for you;
- enjoy staying focused during and after the process of stopping;
- celebrate every step you take;
- really enjoy the benefits of being a non-smoker long after quitting.

If you can bring about your failure, you can bring about your success.

Your own, personal programming

We've all been 'programmed' in our lives to behave in certain ways and, as a result, accidentally or otherwise, we have all kinds of fears and self-doubts. You might think or believe you can't do certain things or deal successfully with various challenges in your life, so you avoid them – and this might include stopping smoking. Or maybe you make attempts to quit, but unconsciously believe, every time, that you'll fail, as you've done in the past. If this has been your experience, you'll know these beliefs merely serve to increase your own poor opinion of yourself – and affect your ability to stop smoking successfully. This could be a way that you've unconsciously programmed yourself to fail. In doing so, you ignore your enormous potential for cultivating and harnessing your own success.

Run a new programme: be the way you want to be. Instead of thinking or feeling you 'can't' stop smoking, why not run a completely new programme and, with the help of this book, learn how to 'ground' and anchor this in your life. This will enable you to resolve past or present conflicts around quitting and to deal with self-sabotage.

'As you change your mind you change your experience', Serge Kahili King, *Kahuna Healing* (Quest Books, 1983)

You're in charge

In fact, you're about to be in charge of managing yourself in a way that's probably very different from anything you've done before. Being in charge of your own actions also means you'll be responsible for the final outcome – successful, content and delighted with yourself.

Stress-management toolkit

If you decide your goal is to stop smoking, the stress-management toolkit presented in Part 2 will help you achieve this as easily and fully as possible. I've adapted and developed these techniques, originally passed to me by Ken and Elizabeth Mellor, international educators, based on teachings that promote well-being, which have been handed down through thousands of years – a fairly solid endorsement!

Learning and mastering the techniques taught in Part 2 – grounding, visualizing, centring, unifying, relaxing – will do the following for you:

• enable you to deal with the challenges ahead;
• tap into your own ability to make the changes you want;
• make things as easy and enjoyable as possible;
• resolve any mixed feelings you have about quitting (including getting 'stuck', self-sabotage and repression);
• enhance your ability to calm yourself and reduce stress levels in a way you think smoking does for you;
• learn how to stay motivated and feel really good about yourself and what you're doing;
• learn how to keep yourself on track;
• learn how to relax naturally.

How will it help me stop smoking?

Why, you might ask, should these methods help when you've tried to stop smoking before and – like so many other quitters – have failed? Past quit attempts may have failed because you have not dealt with your doubts and feelings – especially your feelings of fear. The techniques presented here help digest and manage these feelings in a very effective way. Instead of fighting, ignoring, repressing or denying the urge to smoke, as you may have done in previous attempts to quit, you'll learn how to accept and deal with the urge in relaxed and pleasant ways. These ways will hugely increase your chances of success.

Did you know? You're far more in control of your life – and your addiction – than you realize.

MAKING THE DECISION: FRESH-AIR EXERCISE

1. Take a deep breath of fresh air, hold it for a second, then breathe out. Hear yourself draw in the breath, really feel the purity and freshness as it enters your lungs and disperses around your body. Picture yourself bounding with energy as a result of doing this. Finally, taste and smell the clarity in everything.

2. Light a cigarette, take a deep breath, hold it, then breathe out. Again, hear the depth of your inhalation, feel the pleasure of the 'hit' at the back of your throat, the 'buzz' that reverberates throughout your body. Finally, taste and smell the familiar pleasure of what you're doing.

3. Keep repeating Steps 1 and 2 until you're clearer about which direction you want to go in.

SELF-COACHING TIPS

• *Take a fresh look at your life, review it and see whether continuing to smoke is in line with what's important to you.*
• *You may already know your decision, but don't force it. Continue to be kind and patient with yourself.*
• *Avoid making commitments or big decisions while you remain uncertain about what to do.*
• *Only make your 'big' decision when you're clear that this is the best thing to do – even if only part of you wants to stop smoking at the moment.*

Commitment scale

How committed are you, at this point in time, to continue staying open to the possibility of stopping smoking?

Rate yourself on a scale of 1 to 10, where 1 is no commitment and 10 is totally committed: 1 2 3 4 5 6 7 8 9 10

3 *What do cigarettes do for you?*

'My true nature is joy. Let it be so. Let everything else revolve around that', Swami Amar Jyoti, *Prayer and Meditation* (Truth Consciousness, 2005)

Welcome to this chapter – and well done for getting this far. I want you to be pleased with yourself because you've every right to be. Getting this far means you're about to lengthen your life. And you're embarking on a way of living much more easily – as you'll discover for yourself. So how about doing something right now to reward yourself?

You're willing to suspend your beliefs about what smoking does for you and to continue to be more objective about your habit, a bit like becoming a non-smoker watching someone else smoke. This is another important step forward. Being able to step back like this means you're already starting to separate yourself from smoking. You may even be wondering more concretely how, as a non-smoker, you'll manage to live without cigarettes.

DID YOU KNOW?
Did you know that each cigarette you smoke deprives you – and every cell, muscle and organ in your body – of around 15 per cent of oxygen? This is replaced by carbon monoxide, the same potentially fatal, poisonous gas that comes out of car exhausts and faulty gas heaters? This gas makes your breathing more difficult, damages the lining of your blood vessels and can cause abnormal heart rhythms – sometimes sudden death; it is firmly linked to coronary heart disease and other circulation problems.

Trying to feel good
Like a non-smoker, you want to feel good about yourself. So you use cigarettes. You know it's a quick, immediate way of helping you cope with the intensity of your feelings. Like 'hard' drugs, smoking is a familiar way

of 'medicating' or numbing yourself to help you deal with a situation – whether it's a reward or a comfort, a means of concentrating or relaxing.

In the short term, a cigarette delivers the 'buzz' you need and helps take the 'edge' off things. Smoking dulls things down and helps reduce your own inner intense feelings – so you're not as frightened, anxious or, for that matter, as loving. This is largely due to the substances and poisons contained in cigarettes.

DID YOU KNOW?

When you smoke a cigarette you inhale more than 4,000 chemicals and gases – including arsenic (a deadly poison), ammonia (bleach), and formaldehyde (used to preserve dead bodies).

SMOKING AFFECTS YOUR RELATIONSHIPS

You probably know that when you dampen down your feelings by smoking, you experience more control over what you're doing. You're no longer at the 'mercy' of your own natural feelings. But there are consequences – and they're not only health-related.

Take a minute to think about how smoking affects your relation-ships. Jot down anything that occurs to you.

_____

_____

_____

_____

As a smoker, your contracted or restricted feelings can also affect your relationships. You can become more attached to the chemicals in your cigarettes than to another person. What's often the first thing you do when you get bad news or feel anxious about something? Or you want to reward yourself or celebrate? As a result of lighting up like this, you are more likely to rely on cigarettes for comfort, company and security. One client told me 'As soon as I got upset, I'd automatically reach for a fag. It got to the stage where I shared less and less of myself and my problems with anyone, especially my partner. Cigarettes came first.'

'Reliance on chemicals prevents us from growing and healing', Jon Kabat-Zinn, *Full Catastrophe Living*

Your little 'friends'

In this way, your cigarettes become your 'friends'. You rely on them to help you deal with your emotions (as if somehow the cigarette is able to do this for you), rather than dealing with your feelings yourself or with someone else's help. When this happens, you can inadvertently cause major problems in communication with your partner or friends because you exclude them from a level of intimacy, which you seek instead from a cigarette. Sounds familiar? Next time you reach for a cigarette in a crisis, ask yourself what sort of 'friend' is it that can distance you from those closest to you – and has a 50 per cent chance of killing you.

'Instead of relying on external stability for a sense of security, we need to find security and balance within ... accept change and intensity as normal ... and develop our inner capacities for doing this', Ken and Elizabeth Mellor, educators and therapists

YOUR INNER SECURITY

You can learn to find security within yourself. As part of this process, make a list of feelings and characteristics that you attribute to cigarettes. Start each one with 'Cigarettes help me . . . '

1. Cigarettes help me _____
2. Cigarettes help me _____
3. Cigarettes help me _____
4. Cigarettes help me _____
5. Cigarettes help me _____
6. Cigarettes help me _____
7. Cigarettes help me _____
8. Cigarettes help me _____
9. Cigarettes help me _____
10. Cigarettes help me _____

As an ex-smoker, my list would probably have included: 'achieve a sense of well-being and balance', 'relax', 'concentrate', 'punctuate my day', 'reward myself', 'have time out'.

You are likely, as I did, to believe these 'powers' are inherent in cigarettes. But that belief is an illusion. A myth. The source of that power is in you – not in cigarettes. Believing otherwise means you diminish a belief in your own capacity to solve problems or enjoy yourself fully.

Now ask yourself:
Do you want to rely on cigarettes to get you through for the rest of your life?

- Yes
- No

Damping down emotions

How come we all deal differently with emotions and with intensity? Some people are more open and embrace it, others – especially smokers – tend to contract and try to control it. We all learned particular ways of coping with our emotions as we grew up; we needed to find strategies for dealing with these emotions as a way of managing ourselves – including the need to 'dampen down' or 'control' them. Cigarettes often met this need. In 'trying' to live more easily with ourselves, what we couldn't know at the time was not only how smoking would seriously affect our physical health, but also the health-related quality of our lives.

DID YOU KNOW?

In a recent study of almost 83,000 people in the USA it was found that the current smokers among them (22.4 per cent) were more likely to drink heavily, to binge drink and to report depressive and anxiety symptoms. Additionally, current smokers were significantly more likely than those who never smoked to be physically inactive, to report frequent sleep impairment, frequent pain, and to eat less than five servings of fruits and vegetables per day (GLOBALink, March 2005).

I don't want to be seduced any more

Maybe you're fed up with smoking. It no longer has that cool, sophisticated image.

Maybe you're feeling a bit foolish for carrying on smoking as your friends and work colleagues quit and it becomes increasingly less socially acceptable.

Maybe you're starting to realize the image is just a myth – a way that cigarette companies have managed to deceive and seduce you and other smokers into believing that smoking enhances your looks and lifestyle so they can make lots of money out of you.

Another very successful year

According to ASH (Action on Smoking and Health) at least £9.5 billion a year goes into the treasury from tax on cigarettes – £26 million a day. Cigarette companies make even bigger amounts in profit out of you. Despite their deception about the dangers to health being exposed in the courts, tobacco profits soared by 40 per cent in 2003. Bristol-based Imperial, which is behind the Embassy and Lambert & Butler brands said its share of the home market had risen to 44 per cent after 'another very successful year'.

'If they've got mouths, we want them.' A Marlborough marketing strategy, aimed at the Third World, where 6 per cent of 13-year-olds are addicted to nicotine.

How do you feel after reading this statement? Angry? Reluctant? Accepting? Powerless? Indifferent? Circle the words that apply most.

Sleazy tactics

The secret and 'sleazy' tactics used by the world of tobacco advertising to ensnare the young and manipulate adults were exposed recently. The Cancer Research UK Centre for Tobacco Control, at Strathclyde University in Glasgow, has created the first Internet database of 'evidence', showing how the tobacco industry 'cynically' promotes products that kill 13,000 Scots each year.

Documents reveal strategies to 'grab them young': 'We want to see B&H in the Ben Sherman shirt pockets of Brit-popped, dance-crazed, tequila-drinking, Nike-kicking, "Fast Show"-watching, *Loaded*-reading, babe-pulling, young gentlemen.' And in a letter, an insensitive executive signs off saying: 'Keep smiling, no one's going to die.' (GLOBALink, November 2003).

Cigarette companies knew decades ago that smoking could kill but continued to deceive the public by deploying unscrupulous marketing methods and clever, scientific data to conceal their findings. And the public continued to allow itself to be seduced by advertising with the promise of a cool, sexy image and racy lifestyle.

Interestingly, at the same time scientists were beginning to discover the appalling truth about smoking in the 1950s – when most British adults smoked – the welfare state was being funded almost single-handedly by the tobacco companies. Fifty years later, 'citing new evidence, the Justice Department asserts in more than 1,400 pages of court documents, that the major cigarette companies are running what amounts to a criminal enterprise by manipulating nicotine levels, lying to their customers about the dangers of tobacco and targeting children in their multi-billion dollar advertising campaigns.' (GLOBALink, March 2003).

Is there such a thing as a safe cigarette?

People are still being manipulated by tobacco companies. An article in the *Observer* a few years ago (11 June 2000) posed the question 'Is there such a thing as a safe cigarette?' Who do you believe?

'"Yes", says the Tobacco Company, "We know because we've made one … (it) may present smokers with less risk of cancer, chronic bronchitis and possibly emphysema than other cigarettes … it contains 80 per cent lower levels of carcinogens in smoke and produces 90 per cent fewer skin tumours in mice; 70 per cent less exposure to DNA-damaging chemicals as measured in smokers; 46 per cent less bronchial inflammation and 36 per cent less inflammation of the lower lung."

"No", says Quit, "We'd welcome anything that reduced the health risks of smoking … there is not enough evidence to prove its benefits and the evidence is backed by the tobacco industry, which doesn't exactly have the best record. After all, many people continued smoking because the tobacco industry said the health risks weren't as bad as the scientists said – yet now we know they were … Low tar cigarettes were marketed as safer cigarettes because they provided less of the tar that caused health problems. But it was found that smokers smoked harder and inhaled deeper than predicted, thereby negating any benefits."'

Are you convinced there's a 'safe' cigarette?
• Yes
• No

DID YOU KNOW?

Not only does smoking kill about half of all smokers, it also kills almost half the population in some parts of the UK: 43 per cent of deaths in people over 35 in north Liverpool were due to smoking, according to recent statistics.

What's your initial reaction to reading this fact? Anger? Disbelief? Denial? Disinterest? Anxiety? Shock? Circle the words that apply most.

In what ways do you deny the facts to yourself, or deceive yourself, in the same ways as the tobacco companies do to the public?

It's great you're starting to think in a more open way about smoking and what it does for you. By doing so, you're also opening up to the idea of managing your emotions, as well as the quality of your health, more directly yourself.

'Positive' pays off

We relate better to images of health, rather than illness and disease that smoking can cause; it's far more effective to have a positive view of your body and imagine it working well – seeing 'clear, pink lungs' and feeling your 'easy breathing', than fighting with negative images of addiction, which is why a lot of advertising doesn't work. It generally tends to create guilty or rebellious smokers.

'Smokers will soon be confronted with gruesome images of mouth cancer, gangrenous feet, rotting tongues and diseased lungs on every pack of cigarettes as part of a new 'in your face' anti-smoking campaign.' (GLOBALink, February 2006).

'"Warnings on tobacco product packaging have been telling us the dangers for more than 30 years" said the Australian Health Minister's Secretary. "Sadly, very few realize the full extent of the illness and disease which smoking causes."' (GLOBALink, February 2006)

Confused?

Confusion at this stage can be common. Many smokers suddenly find they become confused about whether or not they really want to stop smoking and whether it is still worthwhile. If you feel like this, keep practising the 'fresh-air' exercise on page 27.

Use your confusion to nurture yourself. Respect your resistance: it's letting you know that you're not fully clear about your decision yet.

Stay open to possibilities and opportunities for positive change. For example, notice small things or events, little 'signals' connected with your smoking going on within you or around you. Perhaps a friend wants to quit as well, or a smoker you know has had a health scare, or you're having more frequent thoughts about quitting, or you've got an opportunity to do something that costs the money you'd save by stopping smoking. Make a note of these signals. (If you don't notice any, then write 'None'.)

_____

_____

_____

_____

It's worth remembering that emotions don't only happen, they are also reinforced – by you. When you keep telling yourself that you can only feel good with a cigarette, that's what you experience. This message gets anchored in the brain and actually changes its structure (see page 16).

SELF-COACHING TIPS

Useful 'external' clues that help you understand your own position better at this stage are envy and anger. Do you sometimes envy quitters – especially friends or work colleagues who have stopped smoking successfully? 'I could do that, if only ... I could have a holiday/had a less stressful job/had a good relationship with my wife, etc. Maybe you feel angry with them: 'How dare they quit without telling me!?'

If this is the case, that's great. Turn it around and use your envy or anger positively: see them as your role models. (You don't have to tell them – keep it a secret if you prefer.) Their success only affects you because part of you wants to achieve the same thing.

Commitment scale

How committed are you, at this point in time, to continue preparing yourself for stopping smoking?

Rate yourself on a scale of 1 to 10, where 1 is no commitment and 10 is totally committed: 1 2 3 4 5 6 7 8 9 10

4 Smoking causes stress

'The very substances we seek out to relieve stress are also stressors on the body in their own right: nicotine and other chemicals in smoke have been implicated in heart disease, cancer and lung disease', Jon Kabat-Zinn, *Full Catastrophe Living*

Having explored in the previous chapter what cigarettes do for you – and to you – you may need time to reflect on this. After all, like most smokers, you probably firmly believe – or believed – that nothing compares with smoking and that an alternative certainly won't do 'the job'.

The comfort zone
Let's continue exploring what smoking means to you at the moment. Smoking usually means staying in charge, staying cool, staying the same. Above all, it's a way of relaxing. The absence of cigarettes would mean cravings and this, in turn, would mean you're not in control. In many ways, it's easier to stay in your 'comfort zone'. Sound familiar? Are you starting to move out of your comfort zone?
• Yes
• No
If 'Yes', what is changing, or has changed?

_____

_____

_____

_____

If nothing comes to mind, what was the discomfort that drew you to this book?

_____

_____

_____

_____

An alternative to smoking

What if you were offered an alternative to smoking? An alternative that:

- helps you in the same ways you think smoking does;
- enhances your own natural capacity to feel calm and relaxed;
- enables you to enjoy life better and to cope more easily with things;
- raises your self-esteem;
- makes you feel good about yourself;
- has the approval of others;
- doesn't cost you anything;
- doesn't harm or kill you.

'CIGARETTES HELP ME RELAX'

'Cigarettes help me relax'. You may have listed this in the exercise in Chapter 3. 'It helps me cope with stress and keeps me calm. And I enjoy it.' To understand your habit of smoking, you need to understand your addiction. How much do you really know about what happens when you smoke? And what do you perceive to be true (as opposed to what is actually true)?

How does smoking relax you?

_____

_____

_____

_____

Do you know what's going on in your brain when you smoke?
- Yes
- No

Did you know that smoking actually causes stress?
- Yes
- No

Smoking causes stress

When we're stressed, our brains release serotonin – our own, natural stress buster. However, smoking inhibits this natural process, so you become deficient in the very substance that would help keep you calm. As a result, smokers are less able to cope with the everyday pressures of life, suffering higher levels of stress than non-smokers.

Now, this seems contradictory. Smoking, as you know from your own experience, does provide some relief from anxiety. You feel contented and happy. But only for a very short time. This is because nicotine temporarily increases levels of dopamine, the 'happy', 'pleasure' or 'sex, drugs and rock 'n' roll' hormone. The irony is that smokers need nicotine to get temporary relief from anxiety and stress, partly caused by smoking itself.

When you're extremely upset or traumatized, the stress-induced effects of smoking are more severe because your brain needs even higher levels of serotonin to help your body cope. So, contrary to what many smokers believe, nicotine's action only makes the situation worse.

Addiction

The main point about dopamine is that smoking stimulates the pleasure or reward centre of the brain. Smoking is like hunger, thirst or lust. You – or your brain – wants to return to the place of pleasure. Remember the unpleasant aspects of smoking when you first started – the coughing, the burning throat, the foul taste, the smoke in your eyes? In fact, there was no pleasure at all to start with. Peer pressure probably drove most of us on, so that eventually the social acceptability, the persistence, the desire to be seen as grown up and no longer a child, all dovetailed neatly with the very powerful addiction of nicotine that soon 'rewarded' you.

This addiction, which many of us toyed with as kids and teenagers, is now regarded as the most powerful and deadly addiction known to man.

SMOKING AND STRESS

So does smoking actually relieve your stress?

• Yes

• No

Let's put it another way. You've probably noticed what happens in the absence of cigarettes: you're likely to experience anger, frustration and cravings; in other words, smoking actually causes stress.

• True

• False

Does smoking help you relax?

• Yes

• No

What happens to your breathing when you smoke? You tend to breathe deeply and this helps deal with stress. But it's the deep breathing – and not the smoking – that helps you relax.

Does smoking actually make you calm?

- Yes
- No

Short-term mood boost

What happens to your mood when you smoke? You may feel good for a short time. This is because nicotine presses the 'happy' hormone button and gives very short-term relief from anxiety and stress. But, far from inducing calm, smokers need nicotine to get temporary relief from the stress that smoking has helped set up in the first place.

What if you could get a similar effect in another way? A way that induces the same sorts of feelings in you as cigarettes, a way that helps you to:

- relieve stress and anxiety;
- keep calm;
- relax;
- concentrate;
- 'reward' yourself;
- punctuate your day;
- quell the agitation that quitters often experience in the first few days or weeks after stopping.

Focusing your thoughts

You may still be unclear about whether or not you want to stop smoking. Put that thought 'on hold' and begin thinking and acting as if you've already decided to go ahead – and just see what happens.

Commitment scale

Bearing this in mind, how committed are you, at this point in time, to continue preparing yourself for stopping smoking?

Rate yourself on a scale of 1 to 10, where 1 is no commitment and 10 is totally committed: 1 2 3 4 5 6 7 8 9 10

5 *Nicotine: good news, bad news*

'We are what we repeatedly do', Aristotle, Greek philosopher

Well done for staying on board. I hope you're treating yourself in small ways every day and noticing the progress you're making, whether that's just by working with this book or in other ways as well. Perhaps you've already stopped smoking? That's great. Being committed to staying stopped is all part of the process of quitting. Knowing about nicotine and what it does to you is another important part of the motivating process. You may not want to know the facts, but it's good to have the information so you know what you're doing to your body.

Good news
I'll start with the good news as it's rather brief. Nicotine's the oily, colourless compound contained in tobacco that the smoker becomes addicted to. Although it enters your body very quickly, taking 7 seconds to reach your brain, it also leaves your body very quickly. In fact, it starts to leave as soon as you extinguish your cigarette.

This is good news, because within 72 hours your body is almost entirely free from nicotine – the addictive part of the cigarette. This means that the physical effects of withdrawal pangs are – or can be – very mild, even though it can take a while for the body to reach a new chemical balance.

Bad news
This information will take a bit longer to tell you about. Nicotine is the fastest addictive drug known to humans – it acts more rapidly than heroin injected into a vein. So just one puff can be enough to become hooked – a fact you may know is true because you've probably experienced it yourself in previous quit attempts – the 'Sod it. I'll just have one' syndrome.

Nicotine is not only a powerful drug – it's also a powerful poison. It's used in insecticides and weed killers. If all the nicotine content in just one cigarette were injected in one go into your vein, it would kill you. But the way nicotine is delivered to you – gradually through each puff – means that doesn't happen. Ironically, nicotine is the relatively 'safe' part of the cigarette compared to the 4,000 accompanying chemicals and gases.

Each time you take a drag, nicotine travels via your lips, mouth, throat and oesophagus into your lungs and then your bloodstream. Seconds later it reaches your brain. If you smoke 20 cigarettes a day and take 20 drags on each one, you are delivering 400 hits of nicotine directly to your brain each and every day.

When you extinguish your cigarette, the nicotine starts to leave your body. You gradually begin to experience withdrawal pangs for more nicotine because the levels in your bloodstream drop down quickly – to about half in 30 minutes and about a quarter in an hour. The reason most smokers light up at least once an hour (or more often) is mainly to avoid withdrawals. The more cigarettes you smoke, the faster this whole cycle becomes.

'In a society that almost demands life at double time, speed and addictions numb us to our own experience', Jack Kornfield, *A Path with Heart* (Bantam USA, 1993)

DID YOU KNOW?

Tobacco smoke contains many other poisons, including carbon monoxide. Some of the effects of these poisons include asthma, angina, bronchitis, lung cancer, heart attacks, disease leading to blindness, infertility, causing the impairment of the development and health of foetuses, and there are the potentially fatal effects of passive smoking on those nearby.

Dr Jamie Inglis, a director with NHS Health Scotland said: 'There are 13,000 deaths a year; 30 per cent of heart disease is caused by smoking and the hospital bill is £200 million' (GLOBALink, November 2003).

DID YOU KNOW?

Every year smoking kills more people than deaths from alcohol, heroin, all drugs, HIV, AIDS and road traffic accidents put together and will kill one in two users when used as intended. In the UK alone, that's at least 320 deaths a day, 120,000 a year.

Nicotine addiction makes it hard to stop smoking. By the time you've had your fourth cigarette, 90 per cent are hooked; by the time you've had your sixth cigarette, 96 per cent are hooked

How many cigarettes do you actually enjoy?

People continue to smoke – often without enjoying it. 'It's just a habit', you say, and often find yourself lighting up without consciously thinking about it. So how many do you really enjoy? How many cigarettes did you actually enjoy today, or yesterday? And which ones? Your fourth cigarette? Your 11th? Your 17th?

Can you name another situation in your life where you habitually repeat something about which you have little or no memory, which you only sometimes enjoy, which stains your teeth, causes your breath and your clothes to stink, which incurs hostility and discrimination, which often forces you outdoors in all weathers, which costs you a fortune and which has a 50 per cent chance of killing you?

The main or primary reason you smoke is not because you enjoy smoking but to top up your nicotine levels. Most smokers need to do this regularly to avoid experiencing withdrawal.

DID YOU KNOW?

Fifty per cent of smokers light up their first cigarette within half an hour of waking up.

Dr Feelgood

When you smoke, you're not just topping up your nicotine levels to avoid withdrawal symptoms as mentioned earlier. You also (as you know) experience pleasure. Once the nicotine has reached your brain, it latches onto a complex receptor known as the nicotinic acetylcholine receptor, or nACh, which triggers the release of dopamine.

Dopamine, as mentioned, is the body's feel-good drug. Anything you find pleasurable – food, sex, drugs – releases dopamine. So each drag on a cigarette triggers a blissful dopamine jolt. The brain is good at learning and remembering pleasure – especially when withdrawal kicks in. As your dopamine level drops off, it leads to cravings.

Nicotine is a 'clever' drug: the physical addiction it creates fits neatly with the psychological need to re-experience the pleasure of it. And, as a smoker, you're more likely to be aware of the 'pleasure' aspect of smoking than the physical addiction.

Nicotine is also a subtle mood enhancer. You may be aware of this and may use cigarettes to meet your needs by puffing in different ways and at different times of the day.

THE LONG AND THE SHORT OF IT

Have you noticed if you're worried you tend to take long drags?
• Yes
• No
Have you noticed if you're in a social situation you tend to take quick drags?
• Yes
• No

DID YOU KNOW?

Smoking tends to be used compulsively. Most smokers (95 per cent) smoke daily.

DID YOU KNOW?

Once you're a daily smoker, your brain undergoes structural changes and closes down some dopamine receptors that would respond to other pleasurable things.

Keeping your levels up

As a smoker, you regulate your smoking habit to maintain your nicotine levels. To illustrate this, take a look at those who smoke 'low tar' cigarettes. It was found they alter their smoking pattern to maintain a desired nicotine intake, known as compensation. So although the cigarettes they smoke contain less tar, they may smoke more cigarettes per day, inhale more deeply, decrease the time between puffs, or cover the air holes in the low tar cigarette that otherwise dilute the smoke delivered to the smoker.

Begin to notice your own patterns of smoking, how your body determines when and how you smoke.

NICOTINE, THE DRUG

Do you see any similarities in the list below between your nicotine addiction and a 'hard' drug – say, heroin? Tick any of the following that apply to both:

• Mostly hooks kids while they are young.
• Associated with rebellion.
• Creates – or can create – a lifelong dependency in a very short time that appears to be hard to break.
• You can usually only score from a supplier.
• Causes you agitation and frustration, possibly trauma, if supply not available on demand.
• Can create a financial drain on the 'consumer', who may choose to buy the drug instead of food.
• Helps you through life by 'numbing down' your emotional responses.
• Makes you feel good for a short while.
• Drains you of your life force and energy.
• Affects others near to you – often causing upset and anger among family, friends and others.
• You find yourself feeling touchy about it, and at other times apologizing for it.
• Often requires you to make breaks from the company you're in to 'disappear' for a 'fix'.
• Often causes lifelong regret.
• Enables others to make huge profits out of you – and has them laughing all the way to the bank.

Which drug do you consider is more addictive and likely to kill you?
• Nicotine
• Heroin

Who's in charge?

When you light up, you may think you're in charge of your smoking and that you decide when you're going to have your next cigarette – but actually, smoking (like heroin addiction) is in charge of you. When the nicotine levels in your body need topping up, you experience withdrawal symptoms: cravings, bad mood, anxiety, increased appetite. So you light up to avoid the symptoms.

Imagine, next time you light up, you had a boss who pressurized you into making him or her a cup of tea 20 times a day. Then ask yourself how come you don't feel similarly resentful at the same internal pressure that comes from you to light up 20 times a day. And if you do feel resentful at having to do this, how come you don't do something about it?

The answer to this question is that as a smoker, you soon realize that you're never free. You need nicotine to function normally. And when the psychological dependence kicks in – like you think you can't concentrate without a cigarette, or life would never hold the same pleasures again – you tell yourself you can't live without it.

Giving yourself a 'fix'

When you top up your nicotine levels or give yourself a 'fix' of nicotine to avoid withdrawal symptoms, you attribute 'feeling good' to the cigarette. You begin to associate 'feeling good' with smoking. How else can you feel this good? And that's the scary bit – you associate being without cigarettes with feeling deprived.

So three things to ask yourself are:

1. How did I cope before I smoked?
2. How do non-smokers cope?
3. How come I don't feel happier?

How we see ourselves

According to psychologist Oliver James, smokers are twice as likely as non-smokers to be depressed – and depression correlates with low levels of the brain chemical serotonin. Many people unconsciously medicate their low serotonin levels by taking 'drugs of solace' – nicotine, alcohol, ecstasy (which, as you now know, just makes things worse).

The important thing is that serotonin levels in the brain are influenced by outside events – including how we perceive our social status – and therefore our happiness.

Research conducted over the past 20 years at the University of California shows that dominant male monkeys have higher levels of serotonin than subordinate ones. (Could this explain why smoking these days is largely an addiction of people in the lower economic income brackets?)

When the going gets tough

'Smoking in films these days is left mainly to the bad guys, the failures and low-lifes, who light up when the going gets tough', the *Guardian*, 9 August 2005

According to researchers who studied 447 films, 48 per cent of characters who smoked were in the lower socio-economic class. The message is that unsuccessful and unglamorous characters reach for cigarettes, winners reach for the stars.

Focusing your thoughts

• When you think about nicotine and what smoking is doing to you, remember the good news: you're classed as a non-smoker when you've stopped smoking for three days. This is the time it takes for most of the nicotine to leave your body.

• You can still experience the feel-good factor in life without cigarettes because your body continues to produce dopamine, so it's important to find other ways of achieving this.

• Instead of reaching for a cigarette to experience pleasure, you can learn to put something else in its place. After all, it's probably the effect of the cigarette you want, not necessarily the cigarette.

'Where I start is (likely to be) where I finish, unless I change my goal', Ken Mellor

SELF-COACHING TIPS
• *Using the information in this chapter – to inform, encourage and enlighten you – is a great way to empower yourself.*
• *Seek out inspiration and question old concepts and beliefs. In the process, you will help yourself make different choices.*
• *Think about ways you can practise boosting your own serotonin levels to develop higher self-esteem.*

DID YOU KNOW?
According to a recent survey by ASH, 'thousands of internal tobacco industry documents released through litigation and whistleblowers

reveal the most astonishing systematic corporate deceit of all time. Publicly the industry... continues to deny that... smoking causes lung cancer – yet it has understood the carcinogenic nature of its product since the 1950s.'

'Until recently, the [tobacco] industry has denied its product is addictive. Most recently it has used a definition of addictiveness so broad that it encompasses shopping and the Internet. Internally, it has known since the 1960s that the crucial selling point of its product is the chemical dependence of its customers. Without nicotine addiction there would be no tobacco industry. Nicotine addiction destroys the industry's PR and legal stance that smoking is a matter of choice.' (ASH website, June 2006)

Commitment scale

How committed are you, at this point in time, to continue preparing yourself for stopping smoking?

Rate yourself on a scale of 1 to 10, where 1 is no commitment and 10 is totally committed: 1 2 3 4 5 6 7 8 9 10

6 *Watch your language*

'Your own words are the bricks and mortar of the dreams you want to realize. Your words are the greatest power you have. The words you choose and use establish the life you experience', Sonia Choquette, *Your Heart's Desire* (Piatkus, 1999)

Well done for persevering with each chapter and for getting this far. This is the last chapter in Part 1 and I hope the information, tips and techniques so far have encouraged, challenged, inspired and excited you and that the experience nourishes and sustains you when you're ready to move on to Part 2: the 'toolkit for success', where many of these ideas are put into practice.

The power of 'never', the power of 'can't'
Lots of smokers say things like 'I'd really like to stop smoking, but I know I'll never be able to have a drink without a cigarette'. Or 'I can't stop smoking. I've tried so many times.' They constantly tell themselves they 'can't' relax without a cigarette, 'can't' think without a cigarette or 'can't' talk on the phone without a cigarette. (I know, I used to do the same thing.)

Where we start is where we finish
I had a client who started off by saying she 'couldn't' have a drink without a cigarette. During our telephone sessions she was able to tailor her smoking to suit her needs: cut down gradually, delayed her first cigarette until later each day, made certain places 'no smoking zones'. But the reason she failed to quit was because she continued telling herself from the outset, she 'couldn't' have a drink without a cigarette. And 'proved' it to be true. She was able to alter everything else about her smoking, except the pattern of associating smoking with drinking and relaxing. Being aware of the power of your language can strongly influence your outcome.

'The maintenance of one's personal power is fundamental to well-being', Michael Harner, *The Way of the Shaman* (Harper Collins, 1990)

Can't stop, won't stop

What do you think is the difference between 'can't' and 'won't'? When someone says 'I can't stop smoking', I challenge them because:

1. It's such a powerfully hypnotic statement. Your brain is busy, as usual, registering it as 'true' every time you say it.

2. It's inaccurate: you can (physically) stop smoking. 'I *won't* stop smoking', is more accurate and has quite a different meaning: 'I'm choosing not to stop smoking'.

3. It's very disempowering to say 'can't', as you're suggesting to yourself – and others – that quitting is beyond your control. On the other hand, 'I won't stop smoking' suggests you have a choice – and that you're choosing not to quit.

'We live by myths that lie so deep we believe them to be reality', David Suzuki, *The Sacred Balance* (Greystone Books, 1997)

The myth of 'can't' in relation to quitting is everywhere – in the media, articles and advertising. In particular, NRT (such as patches or gum) carries with it the message that quitting is 'difficult' and you shouldn't attempt to quit without NRT.

However, those quitters who buy NRT 'over the counter', and don't have additional support and counselling, are only marginally more successful than those who go 'cold turkey' (around 4–5 per cent compared with around 3 per cent at a year).

THE POWER OF LANGUAGE

Give some thought to your use of language (the words you use to describe yourself in relation to smoking) and encourage yourself to think about your *choice* of words, how these might affect you and the way you generally think, act and feel when it comes to smoking.

To help you realize how powerful your choice of words is, look at the two lists on the following page. Focus of the power of language and its effect on you – including your body and your mood.

'For those addicted to their daily dose of nicotine, stopping smoking is as difficult as giving up heroin.' (S. Lonsdale, the *Independent*, 2 January 1996)

You can stop smoking relatively easily with virtually no side effects. The symptoms of withdrawal are manageable and, after the first few days, many say, hardly noticeable.

'Even after the physical cravings have abated, the psychological ones remain.' (S. Lonsdale, the *Independent*, 2 January 1996)

Recent scientific evidence supports the exact opposite: addiction is both physical and emotional and shares the same pathways in the brain; you can desensitize yourself and vice versa.

'It is common knowledge that going "cold turkey" is highly traumatic and probably means you will fail.'

The number of smokers who go 'cold turkey' is hugely under-reported, therefore perceived to be ineffective compared to use of NRT. In fact, the difference is minimal.

'Know that you will become ill with chest and nasal infections.' (S. Lonsdale, the *Independent*, 2 January 1996)

Getting a cough or cold when quitting can actually be a good sign, as it means the lungs are now able to do their job properly. When you smoke, the little hairs or cilia that guard your lungs get clogged up and paralyzed with tar from toxic gases in smoke. Quitting frees them and helps clear out the gunge in your lungs, which can manifest as a cough.

'Here is an infallible way to give yourself some extra willpower in the fight against nicotine' (an advert) and 'Giving up smoking is not easy, but if you've decided you REALLY want to quit, half the battle is won.' (Health promotion)

Willpower is a waste of time. It sets up an internal struggle so all your energy goes into the 'fight'; it's not the cause of failure to quit. Instead, you can learn how to release yourself by focusing on the freedom that resolving any inner doubts can bring.

'It's never too late to try to give up smoking.' (Health promotion)

'Trying' to give up smoking suggests you probably won't succeed. Imagine your pilot announcing he was 'trying' to land at Heathrow. Changing what you say can help change the way you think.

'I get really stressed out just thinking about stopping smoking.'

You can 'programme' yourself to think and behave positively so you end up with what you want, not what you don't want.

'I lost my baby, and because of one doctor's opinion that I had suffocated her in my womb, I was branded a killer' (mother, aged 32, whose daughter's death certificate records 'Still-birth: intra-uterine asphyxia … heavy smoker, 20 a day')

Pregnant mothers need to want to stop smoking not only for their baby's sake but also for themselves.

'We're heading towards the end of January and the pain must really be kicking in now.' (Tom Henry, *Bristol Evening Post*)

Smokers who quit at New Year often do so spontaneously, without realizing you usually need to plan and prepare yourself as fully as possible, including getting help; if you don't cheat within the first week of stopping, you're around 10 times more likely to succeed in staying stopped.

'Once a smoker, always a smoker. I know I will always want another cigarette.'

What you concentrate on is what you get. If you concentrate on freedom and success, that's what you'll experience. Lots of successful quitters are delighted with themselves.

Very few people quit successfully the first time.

Scientific studies show that stopping smoking is more a process than a specific, magical event.

'Counsellors and scientists who study addiction marvel at the iron grip the drug nicotine has on many of its users.'

The number of smokers in England and Wales has hit a record low, with levels now plummeting by 170,000 people each year, according to Cancer Research UK. So welcome! You'll soon be one of the UK's 12 million ex-smokers – if you're not one already.

Which list would you rather read?

Notice the different effects the two lists had on you. Did either list radically affect how you feel about quitting?

Write down three things you noticed about your experience or response.

1. _____
2. _____
3. _____

WORD POWER

Are you aware of how powerful your words are? They can influence your attitudes and decisions – and affect your outcomes. Using words, you can hypnotize or programme yourself into believing certain things are true.

• I'm aware of this
• I wasn't aware of this

There are two ways you can do this:

1. What you say to others. (For example, 'I always end up failing', 'I know it's going to be really difficult'.)

2. What you repeat to yourself. (The 'hidden' power of your inner language like, 'You'll never succeed, you lazy cow!' or 'Here we go again, you bloody loser!')

One way you can help make quitting easier is to talk to yourself and others differently about quitting – especially when it comes to phrases like 'giving up'. Instead of saying 'I'm giving up smoking', experiment with saying 'I'm stopping smoking'.

Do you experience any difference between these two expressions?

• Yes
• No

What is your experience?

_____
_____

WHAT'S IN IT FOR ME?

List the benefits to you of finding an agreeable alternative to smoking that would give you a similar effect without harming you.

1. _____
2. _____
3. _____

Now choose the benefit from the above list that's most important to you, your own reason for wanting to stop smoking. Put it in the present tense instead of the future tense. (Having the verb in the future, keeps it in the future.) For example,

> 'I want to be healthy' becomes 'I am healthy';
> 'I want to be happy' becomes 'I am happy';
> 'I want to be free' becomes 'I am free'.

This sentence is your *affirmation*.

'An affirmation is a strong, positive statement that something is already so', Shakti Gawain, *Creative Visualisation* (Bantam, 1985)

The power of affirmations
It's much better to state what you do want rather than what you don't. Affirmations give your unconscious mind a positive command, so phrase it in the positive, otherwise it won't be 'heard'. The unconscious doesn't register negative commands. So 'Don't talk about smoking' registers as 'Talk about smoking'. And 'I don't want to keep on smoking' wouldn't 'work' because it would register as 'I want to keep on smoking.'

Hold the thought
Having chosen your affirmation, say it to yourself as often as possible, wherever you are – and whatever stage you're at; keep relating to this affirmation as being permanent and experiment with the effects of repeating it. According to the Barefoot Doctor, the most effective way to lodge an affirmation in your unconscious mind, enabling you to override the negative, is to write it down at least six times. It takes six repetitions or more to infiltrate the brain's circuitry, so this is an effective way to 'fix' the idea. So write it down and keep repeating it as often as possible.

1. _____
2. _____
3. _____
4. _____
5. _____
6. _____

Repeat after me

Choose three places where you can repeat your affirmation easily – out walking, swimming, going up and downstairs, cleaning your teeth or washing up. You can get a good rhythm going with any of these activities!

Alternatively, you could write it down over and over again while sitting on a bus or train or lying idly in front of the telly. Use your spare time constructively, as part of your commitment to yourself and your goal.

1. _____

2. _____

3. _____

SELF-COACHING TIPS

• Be aware of the effect words can have on you. And when you notice they are having a negative effect, change them.

• Feel good about getting this far and use your affirmation as a way of helping make your goal a reality, whatever stage you're at. Say it as often as possible, wherever you are, however you may be feeling.

• Build your confidence from the inside out. You'll find that when you start to experience feeling better on the inside, everything will become easier on the outside.

• Go easy on yourself. Change takes time, so it can take you time to start feeling differently about yourself; according to Barefoot Doctor it can take about three weeks of daily affirmation-doing before you begin to see results.

• 'The power of the word is real, whether or not you are conscious of it'. Get into the habit of noticing how powerful your words are – especially words like 'always' and 'never'. Experiment with using other words, like 'sometimes'.

Commitment scale

How committed are you, at this point in time, to continue preparing yourself for stopping smoking?

Rate yourself on a scale of 1 to 10, where 1 is no commitment and 10 is totally committed: 1 2 3 4 5 6 7 8 9 10

PART 2: PREPARATION

7 Step 1: Connecting to your life force

'Our habit energy is strong. That is why we need ... to stop and establish ourselves in the present moment ... Every time it shows its head, pushing us on, we smile to it and it is not able to push us any more. It will go away. Every time we practise this, it loses some of its strength. We don't have to fight it. All we have to do is recognize it and smile at it', Thich Nhat Hanh, *The Path of Emancipation* (Parallax Press, 2001)

Good for you for persevering. You're well on the way to achieving your goal. I hope you're congratulating yourself on your progress and commitment. You may feel it's only a small step in the right direction. But it's also a good and sure way to proceed. Small steps lead to larger ones. So let's keep going.

This chapter is about 'feeling good' and how we try to attain this in different ways, how we manage to effect an altered state of being, for example through various drugs including smoking, and how we can do this naturally in other ways, through processes such as grounding.

COMMITMENT SCALE

First, let's look at your 'commitment scale' ratings. Are you finding they vary? Do they increase steadily or are they quite similar? If you find you're scoring yourself quite high – keep going. If not, do you need to repeat some parts in order to help you be clearer about your goal?
• Yes
• No

Which parts?

_____
_____
_____
_____

Are you finding the scale helpful?
• Yes
• No
If so, how?

_____
_____
_____
_____

If not, what would you find more helpful? Note it here and use it to
help you.

_____
_____
_____
_____

**'Commitment will help unlock your energy to achieve your goal',
Ken Mellor**

Living easily

As humans, we're designed to live easily and in balance and harmony.
So when our feelings flow freely, we naturally tend to feel good about
ourselves. Our bodies work best when we're aware of our physical
selves as well as our physical surroundings.

This is a common experience among quitters who reconnect with
their vitality and their energy. They smile and say things like 'I'm just
so pleased with myself' or 'I feel so much happier' or 'I can do
anything now.'

**'In a state of love, you feel connected and at one with all aspects of
your environment', Barefoot Doctor**

Quitters seem to literally glow with pride and delight when they succeed in stopping smoking. It's as if they have, at last, opened themselves up to life and are living joyfully. They feel free. They say smoking was not, actually, about having a good time. It was more about using a cigarette to try and have a good time – to try and relax, to stop worrying and to enjoy a state of peace and tranquillity that non-smokers can enjoy any time they like. Within a short time of having quit, they struggle to remember the association of cigarettes with pleasure.

Getting closed down

Smoking interrupts this natural process of living more easily. As a smoker, your feelings are often contracted, constricted, closed down – and you tend not to feel as good about yourself a lot of the time. You're aware that you're often lethargic and sluggish. This is because you are exhausting and poisoning your system by smoking, as well as depriving yourself of oxygen and energy. There's a lot of research to support the view that many smokers are depressed. You might use cigarettes to 'feel better'.

The feel-good factor

Smokers often say that lighting up can calm their nerves, satisfy cravings and help them relax. New evidence shows smoking produces major changes in the flow of feel-good chemicals between brain cells – both temporarily and in the long-term. Those changes in flow match up with changes in how smokers say they feel before and after smoking. People have always sought out the 'feel-good' factor to enhance a sense of well-being. As one man in a workshop said, 'We all need a little something'. And he's right.

But should the feeling that you 'need a little something' become worth more than your life? The Minister for Health recently said 'smoking is the only joy some people have' (he himself had only recently quit). What do you think about this?

_____

_____

_____

_____

The universal quest to attain a state of peace, harmony and tranquillity is a very basic, human need. A quick trip around the world shows that most cultures have various ways to meet this need. They include ritual pipe-smoking, chewing leaf tobacco and betel nut, alcohol, and smoking cigarettes, cigars and pipes. Some believe marijuana may soon be legalized in the UK and a minority argue for even harder drugs, such as cocaine and heroin, to be added to the list. All these 'enhancers' provide their consumers with pleasure – and the sensory effects are experienced as a panacea, calming the body and mind, helping them feel good.

Part of the way of life

The most popular 'enhancer' in the UK, particularly in the 1950s, was smoking. And the pleasure of smoking continued unchallenged until evidence connecting it with danger began emerging in the late 1960s. Up until then, almost everyone smoked: half of all women and two-thirds of all men, compared to current statistics of around 23 per cent of women and 25 per cent of men.

Smoking had become part of the British (and Western) way of life. You could smoke anywhere – and people did: at the cinema, in their surgery, in hospital. It was regarded as cool, sexy and 'good' for all sorts of things – including sex and sore throats!

All that has changed. Smoking is far less socially acceptable amongst the majority of the population where the professional classes continue to quit at a much higher rate and health issues around smoking are fast becoming associated with deprivation.

'Risk factors for heart disease such as obesity and smoking are on the increase, especially in deprived communities where people are more likely to smoke and to eat a diet high in saturated fats', Sara Boseley (the *Guardian*, March 2005)

The search for peace and harmony

Although we probably 'all need a little something', it's important to break the association between cigarettes and pleasure and to think about alternatives to the seductive power of smoking. One alternative technique for feeling good is known as 'grounding'. It has been used for thousands of years as a way of helping people to enhance their spiritual well-being and to live more balanced lives.

The great thing about grounding is that it deals with a very basic need in smokers and one of the main reasons they light up: the need to become calm and to establish oneself in the present moment.

Helping anxieties

How often do you light up because you're feeling anxious about something that's happened in the past or might happen in the future?
- Very often
- Often
- Sometimes
- Occasionally

Being grounded helps you deal with this anxiety by bringing you into the present moment: the here and now. By activating your own natural system to help dissolve anxiety – and digest what you're experiencing – you may find, as others have done, that you can handle your worry.

'Only when you truly inhabit your body can you begin the healing journey', G. Roth and J. Loudon, *Maps to Ecstasy: Teachings of an Urban Shaman* (New World Library, 1989)

Grounding doesn't have the same lure, power and seduction as cigarettes, but it's a great way of contributing to your sense of peacefulness and well-being. And, according to many quitters, myself included, it's really helpful in preparing you for the challenges of quitting – and staying quit so 'it's not able to push us any more'. Because our 'habit energy' is very strong, learning how to deal with this strength by being in the present moment is a very effective way of managing addiction.

What is grounding?

Grounding means being aware of your physical sensations and what's going on around you at the same time. It's something you do already – you're probably aware of extreme situations that can prompt a strong physical reaction in you, such as sucking on a lemon, hearing the scrape of fingernails down the blackboard or smelling a rose.

Grounding is a skill you can learn to develop quite easily. It's a great way to release tensions that prevent you from being in your natural state of 'connectedness'.

Natural awareness

Grounding is a simple, natural process. You're grounded when you have some physical awareness of what's happening 'inside' your body at the same time as you're aware of the physical things and events 'outside' or around you. Everyone is grounded to some extent. This awareness may not dominate the rest of your awareness, yet it's there, accompanying everything you're perceiving, regardless of what you're doing. This means you can make plans, enjoy yourself, talk to others, drive a car – do anything – and stay aware.

You already have the ability to ground yourself, so you're not learning anything new, you're simply connecting with a process that is natural to you. Your body will show you the way, if you'll let it do what it's designed to do. You 'ground' yourself in different ways already – by smelling flowers, tasting food, swimming in cold water or pinging a rubber band on your wrist (as a friend of mine did to help her manage panic attacks).

As babies and young children we were naturally well grounded. Like other animals, we were in touch with our physical needs. We cried when we needed something, and were (usually) placated when the crisis was over. Then we automatically and naturally returned to equilibrium.

We were much more in touch with our physical experience back then – our physical connection with the things around us – but we learnt ways to interrupt this ability to some extent as we got older.

'The quieter you become the more you can hear',
Baba Ram Dass

Being in the here and now

Grounding means we're fully present in the moment. We become 'pin-pointed' so that all our strength, vitality and awareness are available to us. Sometimes, when grounded, uncomfortable feelings intensify. If this happens, it's good to persist with grounding. Your body takes care of the rest.

Grounding is a great, natural way to bring yourself into the 'here and now', to change your 'habit energy', and to fully live in the moment by maintaining physical, emotional and cognitive balance and equilibrium – all without harming yourself.

Another huge benefit of living in the present is that this puts you in touch with your natural capacity to experience joy, pleasure and vitality. With grounding, all sorts of things become clearer: communication, intimacy, thinking and digesting feelings.

'The more you concentrate on being at peace with yourself, the more peaceful you'll become', Ken Mellor

DID YOU KNOW?

Some scientists believe that drugs which boost serotonin levels (your own natural means of calming yourself) would be far more effective than nicotine patches in the crucial three weeks following quitting. This is the time it takes the chemical pathways to recover after you quit. (GLOBALink, March 2004).

Have you spotted the link between the ancient technique of grounding and the scientific discovery mentioned above? How about bringing these two things together and creating your own natural calming mechanism? Let's think about using grounding as an alternative to cigarettes and just see what happens.

'This moment is different from any other moment, this moment is perfect. It is now', The Incredible String Band

TOOLKIT FOR SUCCESS EXERCISE 1: GROUNDING

This exercise, like the other toolkit exercises, was passed on to me by Australian meditation teachers Ken and Elizabeth Mellor. As mentioned, it is based on ancient teachings that promote well-being. It is also known as 'Living in the Present'.

Consider the exercise as a fundamental part of your toolkit for success. It's a great way of preparing yourself for quitting by learning how to relax *before* you stop smoking. You can practise it anywhere – sitting, standing or walking, and it only takes a few seconds.

'Master your senses, what you taste and smell, what you see, what you hear. In all things be a master of what you do, say and think. Be free', Buddha

STEP 1

Anchor yourself by maintaining an awareness of the contact you're making with the chair (if you're sitting down) or your feet with the floor (if you're standing up) – or both.

STEP 2

While you're doing that, go inside your body and use your senses to look at, listen to, touch, taste and smell what's going on inside you. Take your time doing this.
• Look at any areas that are light or dark in your body.
• Listen to any sounds or silences in there.
• Feel any areas that are hot or cold, tight or loose, tingling or numb.
• Taste or smell anything there too.
• Notice your physical sensations like this for at least a few seconds; and talk to yourself about what's there.

STEP 3

Now do the same on the outside. Continue anchoring yourself by maintaining your awareness of the contact you're making with what's supporting you. Then use your senses to look at, listen to, touch, taste and smell what's around you. Take your time doing this.
• Look at colours, shapes, patterns.
• Hear the sounds and the silences.
• Feel the texture of something near you: is it rough or smooth, warm or cold?
• Feel the air against your skin.
• Taste and smell anything around you.

STEP 4

Finally, for a minute or two, do them both together, always 'anchoring' yourself first.

Reflection

When you've finished, make a note of your experiences – what, if any, are the differences?

_____

_____

_____

_____

TIPS FOR PRACTISING GROUNDING

• _Notice the areas of your body in which you are comfortable and at ease. If you are very uncomfortable, move your attention to areas where you're not noticing much at all. Moving around definitely helps._

• _Don't worry if you find that your awareness is very subtle – even a small change is enough for you to experience the benefits. Again, your experience can be increased through physical movement._

• _Notice things of beauty and pleasure on the 'outside' and the 'inside'._

• _Move from 'inside' to 'outside' when you want._

Make grounding part of your day

Persevere with grounding: give yourself time and permission to do it regularly every day. Make it part of your everyday life – and notice the differences. It's simple, immediate and automatic. If you find you're putting lots of effort into it, then relax – you may be trying too hard. It's a good idea to anchor these exercises with something you do regularly, as an easy way of helping you to remember to do it. Here are some examples:

• every time you get into your car or sit at traffic lights;
• every time you open and close your front door;
• whenever you're making tea or coffee;
• whenever you get an impulse to light up.

Some people set their watch to go off every hour or so, to remind themselves to ground regularly.

Write down three places, times or situations where you could do the grounding exercise(s) each day.

1. _____

2. _____

3. _____

'We are healed of our suffering only by experiencing it to the full',
Marcel Proust, French author

WHAT'S SO GREAT ABOUT SMOKING?

When you're familiar with grounding, think again about all the reasons you like smoking. Maybe you're smoking now; if not, light up (if that's possible); otherwise, use your memory, and really get into it. Be aware of the whole process from the beginning:

- holding the packet;
- taking out a cigarette;
- picking up the match or lighter;
- the anticipation of pleasure;
- placing the cigarette between your lips;
- lighting it;
- breathing in the smoke;
- experiencing the 'hit' or 'buzz' as you do so;
- breathing out the smoke.

Be aware of how you think that cigarette helps you. Now get yourself well-grounded and make another list of what cigarettes do for you. As on page 30 in Chapter 3, start each reason with 'Cigarettes help me'.

1. Cigarettes help me _____

2. Cigarettes help me _____

3. Cigarettes help me _____

4. Cigarettes help me _____

5. Cigarettes help me _____

6. Cigarettes help me _____

7. Cigarettes help me _____

8. Cigarettes help me _____

9. Cigarettes help me _____

10. Cigarettes help me _____

How is this list different from the one you did on page 30?

_____

_____

_____

_____

What has changed?

_____

_____

_____

_____

Are there any areas that you think you need to attend to?

_____

_____

_____

_____

Life-changing process

Many quitters, when well grounded, have found this simple, natural process enhances their lives considerably. They say it's life-changing and can help in lots of different ways. Circle the points that appeal to you.

- 'It helps me feel calm and relaxed – giving a sense of inner peace.'
- 'I'm less worried and anxious about things.'
- 'Really helps me release troublesome feelings and thoughts.'
- 'Helps me deal with difficult situations more easily.'
- 'Makes good things even better.'
- 'Helps raise my confidence and self-esteem.'
- 'Helped prepare me for the challenges of quitting.'
- 'Makes the process of quitting much easier.'

Clear your mind

Like other smokers, you may still be having doubts about quitting and may be continuing to weigh up the pros and cons. Use grounding to help clarify your thoughts and doubts. Choose something to do with quitting that you're confused about, then focus your attention on your body, using the grounding technique. Do this for a few minutes, then come back to your problem and notice what you're experiencing.

_____

_____

_____

_____

SELF-COACHING TIPS

If you associate cigarettes with relaxing, be aware of this link and change it. Start associating grounding with relaxation instead.

Remember, grounding is life-enhancing, life-affirming. This is partly to do with the way it has the effect of intensifying and spreading feelings of pleasure, comfort and aliveness in our bodies. At the same time, it helps us release and dissolve feelings of discomfort. So use it as often as possible to help you stay concentrated on whatever you're dealing with – and help prepare you for future challenges with ease and optimism.

Being grounded might present you with something else to attend to – for example, you might realize you're feeling bored or lonely. So instead of lighting up, experiment by ringing a friend or doing something other than smoking to meet that need in you.

Commitment scale

How committed are you, at this point in time, to continue preparing yourself for stopping smoking?

Rate yourself on a scale of 1 to 10, where 1 is no commitment and 10 is totally committed: 1 2 3 4 5 6 7 8 9 10

Step 2: Creating what you want for yourself

'To begin making your dream a reality, apply the first principle of Creativity. Focus on what you want to create, give it your full attention and make it your intention to experience it', **Sonia Choquette,** *Your Heart's Desire*

Where do I begin?

You've already begun, so congratulate yourself. Reward yourself. And keep doing so every day. You're about to lengthen your life. You're embarking on a way of living that you'll discover you can enjoy much more easily and fully without cigarettes. Stopping smoking is a process that may be gradual or sudden – one we all go through as smokers before finally quitting. And it can be greatly helped by your ability:

• to experience ease, steadiness and equilibrium through being well grounded;

• to incorporate grounding into the technique shown in this chapter, which is designed to help you create what you want for yourself;

• to imagine yourself as a successful, happy non-smoker.

It's easy

One thing you need to know is this process is easy. You may think it's not. If you've tried to stop smoking before and believe from your own experience, or others', that it's difficult, the internal struggles drain you of energy and this can be irritating, depressing and exhausting. It's like one side is pushing against the other. To help you deal with this, how about thinking of something you do that is easy – like riding a bike, swimming or driving a car. Once upon a time you learnt how to do it and you got through all the challenges. Now you know how to do it automatically. It's no longer an issue for you. Learning how to stop smoking is exactly the same.

'Always begin the process with considering what you want, how you want things to be, what will be happening when everything is as you'd like it to be … and think about them as if they're already accomplished', Ken and Elizabeth Mellor

Most quitters say they found quitting much easier than they thought it would be. One man who attended a workshop said rather crossly 'Why didn't someone tell me it'd be this easy? I've been smoking for 28 years.'

You might be wondering how quitters can say things like that, if you're feeling the exact opposite. You might even think they're lying, because you've persuaded yourself to believe that quitting is difficult. This is understandable as your belief is continually reinforced in the media, with constant images of battles between smokers and cigarettes. But it's important not to confuse the need to persist with certain challenges as evidence that it's bound to be difficult.

'Intention is not wishful thinking … it's like an arrow flying towards a target', Sonia Choquette, *Your Heart's Desire*

Start with your success

Let's start in the same way as you plan to finish, with your success: Imagine you're now at the end of the book.
- You've got what you wanted.
- You enjoyed working your way through it.
- You found the techniques helpful and inspiring.
- You absorbed the tips.
- You repeated exercises until you felt ready to move on.
- You committed yourself to furthering your goal every day.
- And now you've achieved your goal.

And it was so much easier than you thought. You've stopped smoking successfully with absolutely no likelihood of relapse. And you *feel great.*

'You have the power in the present moment to change limiting beliefs and plant the seeds for the future of your choosing. As you change your mind, you change your experience',
Serge Kahili King, *Kahuna Healing*

CREATE YOUR SUCCESS

• Close your eyes and imagine yourself feeling full of energy, enjoying hearing your friends and family congratulate you, seeing yourself glowing with health, smelling and tasting fresh, and being nice to be near. You're free. You feel great.
• Now go inside your body and ground yourself by using all your senses.
• Enjoy your success for a few moments as if it's happening right now.
• When you finish, notice what you're experiencing and make a brief note of it (you can use your imagination here also).

_____

_____

_____

_____

The more you do this little exercise, the easier it will be to imagine your goal – and the easier it'll be to achieve it.

'Life starts moving in the right direction when you put your attention on your Heart's Desire and then make it your intention to create it', **Sonia Choquette,** *Your Heart's Desire*

HOW YOU GET THERE

If you want to achieve your goal of quitting and experience it like 'an arrow flying towards a target', it's important to change the way you think about how you attain that goal. Don't allow yourself to be attached to your fears.

Practising the grounding exercise will help release you by dealing with these feelings. Let's return to the exercise above, where you imagined you'd achieved your goal easily. How did you achieve your goal?
• Easily
• Fairly easily
• With difficulty, but got there in the end
• Didn't really expect to succeed, but gave it a try.
Do you feel the same about your present real-life situation regarding quitting?

- Yes
- No

If 'No', why not?

_____

_____

_____

_____

ACHIEVING THINGS EVERY DAY

Think about how you approach everyday tasks and things you do routinely, like driving a car, cooking a meal or swimming.
How do you usually approach the task?

_____

_____

_____

_____

Do you see its accomplishment as easy and straightforward?
- Yes
- No

What do you usually expect in terms of the outcome?

_____

_____

_____

_____

Now compare doing this routine task with stopping smoking. When you think about setting your quit date, which of these options best expresses how you expect to achieve your goal?
- Easily
- Fairly easily
- With difficulty, but will get there in the end
- Don't really expect to succeed, but will give it a try

Is your answer the same as the one you gave for the routine task you chose, above?
- Yes
- No

If 'No', why not?

_____

_____

_____

_____

'You get the best results by imagining you've already succeeded and that you did so very easily', Ken Mellor

WHAT YOU FOCUS ON, IS WHAT YOU GET

We tend to get what we expect in life. If we expect to succeed, we usually do. Look at your own life: if you expect to succeed (pass exams, get the job you want, enjoy good health and loving relationships), that's probably what happens. If you expect trouble (failing exams, not getting the job you want, things always going wrong, fraught relationships), that's generally what you get. If you want something on the surface, but underneath have doubts, this will also influence the outcome.

How do you usually get things in your life?

• Easily
• Not so easily
• With difficulty
• Not at all.

Whether big or small, think about how much you've already achieved in your life. Note some examples down here.

_____

_____

_____

_____

TOOLKIT FOR SUCCESS EXERCISE 2: CREATING WHAT YOU WANT FOR YOURSELF

'Imagination is not make believe; it's the journey of an unfettered mind', Carl Hammerschlag, _The Theft of the Spirit_ (Fireside, 1994)

The exercise is about using your imagination to help you achieve your goal to stop smoking. With visualization, you need to go for what you want ('I want to be free from cigarettes') not what you don't want ('I don't want to continue smoking'). Put it in the present tense and say 'I am a non-smoker' or, preferably 'I am free', so you're not associating your goal with the word 'smoking'. Remember, putting your affirmation in the future keeps it in the future.

STEP 1

Be clear about your goal: what is it you want to be happening? Imagine you've already achieved your goal and you did so really easily. See yourself as being already stopped, feel your delight, hear the applause, taste and smell the fresh air. The more vivid and vibrant you make your fantasy, the more effective it'll be.

STEP 2

Go for gold by including as much as you can in your imagination. The more you include the better:
- I stopped smoking easily and I am healthy, terrific, clever—
- I smell gorgeous.
- Food tastes fantastic.
- I've got loads of extra money.
- I feel so pleased with myself.
- I know I can do anything now.

Picture this in your mind and really see, feel, hear, taste and smell the truth of this statement. Then enjoy the feelings as if they were true.

STEP 3

Deliberately use 'I am' affirmations to help mobilize your own inner power and resources.
- I am healthy
- I am free
- I am fantastic

The more committed you are, the more successful you'll be – and the more confident you'll be about achieving what you want.

STEP 4

Use grounding. This is important as it helps take care of your feelings so you're balanced and in harmony.

STEP 5

Do something at the end of this exercise as if the whole visualization were true. For example:

- talk on the phone without a cigarette;
- clean out the ashtray in your car and decide to keep it a 'clean air zone';
- freshen your mouth by cleaning your teeth.

This is important because it brings your actions out of fantasy and into reality. It doesn't need to be a big action, just in line with making your goal a concrete reality.

> ### TIPS FOR THIS VISUALIZATION EXERCISE
> 1. Go for what you want.
> 2. Think of your goal as already achieved; keep it in the present tense.
> 3. Only settle for the very best – the 'Go for Gold' picture.
> 4. Use 'I am' affirmations and picture, hear and feel the truth internally.
> 5. Remember to use grounding.
> 6. Do something practical to make your visualization real – like putting ashtrays out of sight.

'To say yes to life is at one and the same time to say yes to oneself. Yes – even to that element ... which is most unwilling to let itself be transformed from a temptation into a strength', Dag Hammarksjold, from *The Adventure of Peace* (Edited by Sten Ask, Palgrave Macmillan, 2006)

FIVE THINGS THAT I AM

Finally, when you've finished, write down five responses about your new status (as if you've already achieved your goal).

1. I am _____
2. I am _____
3. I am _____
4. I am _____
5. I am _____

Choose one of these affirmations and have it at the forefront of your mind. Write it down as often as possible, repeat it frequently, walk to the rhythm of it, see it written above your desk, kitchen sink, TV or computer screen in big letters – 'I am great!', 'I am free!'

Make visualization part of your day

It's a good idea to practise visualization for a few minutes every day as part of your commitment to yourself. Build it into your morning routine – immediately after you get up, before you take a shower, when you're out walking, or anything else you do regularly.

'If you want to develop a new habit attach it to an old one', Anon

The more you practise, the easier your goal becomes and the greater your confidence in bringing it about. Like grounding, you can do visualization in a few seconds with a bit of practice.
Make a note of three times and places you can easily practise:

1. _____
2. _____
3. _____

Do I really want to?

See your goal as something you're creating for yourself; something you intend, from the start, to achieve. Make it your intention to create it. Like other new things in your life, for example learning to drive, you first need to decide whether or not you want to go ahead. This decision can be a stumbling block for smokers: do I really want to?

If you had the same doubts about, say, learning to drive, but decided on balance, to go ahead and learn, what did you do to take care of yourself in the process?

_____
_____
_____
_____

In the same way, if you were sure – or fairly sure – you wanted to go ahead and learn how to stop smoking successfully, what would you do to take care of yourself in the process?

_____
_____
_____
_____

You can experience the same degree of certainty and confidence about quitting as you did about learning to drive and use it to help you achieve your goal.

BE CERTAIN

Fix on something you can see, hear or feel. It might be a picture, a traffic noise out in the street, the texture of something close to hand. Just be aware of the certainty of its existence. Now use that same feeling of certainty to be certain of your own success. You can enhance this feeling by grounding yourself at the same time. Enjoy doing this for a few seconds.
How does it feel?

_____
_____
_____
_____

Commit to success

When you set a goal for yourself, you aim for and expect to achieve that goal. You do everything possible in line with that – regular lessons, studying how to achieve your goal, practising in order to perfect the skill and staying committed. Regular practice will help you perfect your skills in a way that results in you doing it automatically.

Remember that motivation is not the same as commitment; your motivation may waver, but if your commitment stays the same you will reach your goal.

YOU'RE THERE ALREADY

Affirm you're already a non-smoker by regularly doing something in line with your new status to bring your fantasy into reality. Note it down here (for example, drinking tea and holding the cup with both hands).

_____
_____
_____
_____

Change the triggers

Change the 'triggers' that you associate with lighting up. This will help you realize your goal more easily.

- If you smoke first thing, have a shower instead.
- After a meal go for a walk or do the dishes.
- Visit the dentist and get your teeth cleaned and polished.

SELF-COACHING TIPS

- *You can write your own script for success. What you concentrate on is what you get.*
- *If you expect to succeed, you probably will.*
- *If you expect to fail, you probably will.*
- *If you expect to succeed in the end, but also expect it will be difficult, it probably will be.*
- *You get the best results by imagining you've already succeeded and that you did so very easily.*
- *If you're not sure what you want at this stage, imagine it anyway by seeing everything as being perfectly sorted out.*
- *If you experience something you don't want, like self-doubt, turn this around and use it as a trigger to focus on what you do want. Have a little chat with yourself: 'Ah, there goes that feeling of self-doubt – thanks for reminding me. But I want the exact opposite. I want certainty!'*
- *Change your physical environment. Even quite small changes can make a difference. Dump the ashtrays, or decide not to smoke in a particular room.*
- *Learn relaxation or tai chi.*
- *Get into the habit of grounding wherever you are.*
- *Practise the exercise 'Creating What You Want for Yourself' for a few minutes every day, ideally for two to three weeks. Experiment with it and notice the difference. Your goal becomes easier and easier to imagine. Repeat it as often as you can to get the result you want.*

Commitment scale

How committed are you, at this point in time, to continue preparing yourself for stopping smoking?

Rate yourself on a scale of 1 to 10, where 1 is no commitment and 10 is totally committed: 1 2 3 4 5 6 7 8 9 10

9

Step 3: Facing your fears

'The whole point of transforming our heart and mind is to find happiness', The Dalai Lama

How is everything going? I hope you're continuing to congratulate yourself. Your 'commitment scale' responses are your barometer – a clue to the ease you're experiencing around change. Keep going if you're happy with your responses; if not, just repeat the relevant exercises or material until you are.

Fear is often the reason many smokers keep their habit going – fear of failure, fear of not being able to cope, fear that life will never be the same again, fear of losing your 'little friends', fear that you may have to put some effort into stopping smoking.

And that's not all. You may feel increasingly surrounded by things or situations that arouse fear in you such as anti-cigarette campaigns and advertising on TV, social pressures to quit, books and magazine articles, questions from your doctor about your smoking.

WHAT'S THE WORST THAT CAN HAPPEN? PART 1

So what's this fear about? How can you be expected to want to stop smoking without attending to the very thing that may prevent you from quitting in the first place? It's therefore useful to ask yourself 'what's the very worst that can happen?'

What are you afraid might happen if you stop smoking? List three of the worst things that come into your mind.

1. _____
2. _____
3. _____

Quitters usually have one or more of the following thoughts or feelings:
• 'I won't be able to cope without cigarettes.'
• 'I'm afraid I might blow a fuse without cigarettes.'
• 'I'm afraid I might lose my identity, my independence, without cigarettes.'

Getting stuck

If you avoid facing your fears, nothing changes. Instead, you stay 'stuck'. Listing three of your worst fears will help you identify some of the things that keep you stuck and keep you smoking.

Identifying the worrying thoughts and emotions that you associate with stopping smoking is really helpful. Once you're in touch with the feelings aroused by thoughts of quitting, you can start to deal with them. For example, in the above exercise, you may have thought 'How would I cope without a cigarette?' and then experienced a kind of panic. Or maybe you had the panicky feeling first, then realized its cause.

Managing fearful feelings

1. Start to recognize them.
2. Allow yourself to experience the feelings instead of repressing them.
3. Know how to deal with these feelings when they arise, by grounding.

'Live the experience of each moment, whether it's rage, grief, agony or fear; at the same time, it's really important to keep some attention on how you'd like things to be', Ken Mellor

WHAT'S THE WORST THAT CAN HAPPEN? PART 2

Repeat the exercise about listing your three worst fears, this time grounding yourself first.

When you feel well grounded (take your time), fill in the list.

1. _____
2. _____
3. _____

Staying grounded, allow yourself to experience these same fears. Make a note of your experience.

_____
_____
_____

How does the second time differ from the first exercise? If you experience nothing, then keep going until your experience is clearer. If you find the effects are quite subtle, that's fine; it's still effective; keep repeating this cycle.

Turning points

Turning points are those moments when we realize we want to change something, where we start to think, feel or act differently about it. Anticipating any change can be exciting, as well as inducing all kinds of fears in us – especially smokers. You might be wondering and worrying how you'll cope without cigarettes, how you'll concentrate, relax, reward yourself, manage crises, go to the pub, punctuate your day, fill the void.

Quick exercise

'Prove' the change you want is already occurring. Jot down three things you've noticed to support this.

1. _____
2. _____
3. _____

'As you go the way of life, you will see a great chasm. Jump. It is not as wide as you think', Joseph Campbell, American author

Change can be scary

As human beings, instead of embracing change as something natural, we often do the exact opposite: we resist or fear change – often because it represents a loss of structure for us. So we struggle to ignore it by doing things to distract ourselves – like drinking excessively, taking tranquillizers or smoking. This tends to make things needlessly more difficult for us, as our bodies try to tell us. In spite of all that you know to the contrary, you may continue to think you can only cope with certain situations in the same way: through smoking.

'At our core is a place of absolute stillness … when you manage to identify with that nothing can truly rock your boat again', Barefoot Doctor

When smoking is part of your lifestyle, the prospect of changing it by quitting may seem a scary thing to do – even though you want to. You've probably come to rely on cigarettes for lots of reasons, some of them contradictory.

'Even though the rates of change (in the body) may differ, change is always there', Deepak Chopra, *Quantum Healing* (Bantam, 1990)

DID YOU KNOW?

Our bodies, like other forms of life, change over time. They renew themselves frequently: 90 per cent of our cells are replaced every three months.

Renewal

The above fact is brilliant news for smokers. It means you can 're-educate' and influence your body and bathe it in new, positive thoughts, feelings and actions – a whole new programme if necessary – in much the same way we influence the growth of new plants with nutrients in good fertilizer. Our bodies – and our minds – have an amazing capacity for re-establishing health and equilibrium – even if you have been lighting up, maybe twenty times a day, for years.

How are you going to feel?

The following quote helps make sense of statements made by quitters six weeks after quitting. They say things like 'It feels weird to be talking about smoking … I've more or less forgotten about it' or 'It's only while you're addicted that the importance of the addiction can get distorted and exaggerated'. 'Addiction to cigarettes can feel huge', said one client 'and so much bigger than you.'

'If you could see your body as it really is, you would never see it in the same way twice. Ninety-eight per cent of the atoms in your body were not there a year ago . . . It's as if you lived in a building whose bricks were taken out and replaced every year', Deepak Chopra, *Quantum Healing*

Looking back, quitters can't quite believe they were so addicted. It's only when they are 'through' it and have dealt with the addiction that most say they found it 'so much easier' than they thought it'd be.

'If you want something badly enough, you can achieve it', Anon

What we share intensifies

Many quitters tend to express their fears by focusing on the things that are not going well. The effect of doing this can sometimes mean you're setting yourself up to fail. Here's an example:

• You allow yourself to get overwhelmed by a craving.
• You become fearful of not managing the situation well.
• You have a go at someone.
• You feel bad about this and (eventually or quite quickly) see the only solution as having a cigarette.
• You've tried and it's just too difficult.
• You keep telling yourself and others just how difficult it is.

What happens is you don't allow yourself to fully experience the problem – to immerse yourself in it as a way of dealing with it and then letting it go. But when you push it out of the way, fight it, try to ignore it or suppress it, this only strengthens it.

Give one example where you have done the same:

_____

_____

_____

_____

'What you fight, you invite – and make stronger', Ken Mellor

HAVE A GOOD LOOK AT YOURSELF

Let's develop your 'observer'. Get into the habit of consciously noticing what you're doing, feeling or thinking. For example, when you think 'Ooh, I feel like a cigarette', observe what you're experiencing at that point. For example, you might be feeling empty, bored, anxious. Observing yourself in this way helps you become more aware of your cravings and what triggers them. You may still decide to have the cigarette, you may not.

If you are still smoking, record your observations about your next three cigarettes.

1. _____

2. _____

3. _____

TOOLKIT FOR SUCCESS EXERCISE 3: CENTRING

This exercise is useful to help you manage possible cravings – or any other stresses in your life. By practising it, you can guide yourself to 'that place of absolute stillness'. You use the power of being your observer to notice what's there without being thrown by it.

STEP 1
Sit comfortably.

STEP 2
Breathe in deeply and say to yourself: 'I am breathing in life'.

STEP 3
Breathe out and say to yourself: 'I am breathing out anti-life'.

STEP 4
Observe yourself and experience yourself as peaceful, calm, serene.

STEP 5
Centre yourself in 'that place of absolute stillness'.

STEP 6
Ground yourself.

STEP 7
Repeat this a few times and notice any differences.

_____

_____

_____

_____

When you do this exercise, you'll find other things seem less significant. Therefore, when you experience a craving, you won't be overwhelmed by it or think that the only way you can cope is to have a cigarette.

Practise centring as often as you can. You can do it anywhere and everywhere. You'll find it helps you relax as well as connect you with your own, nourishing life force.

TIPS FOR CENTRING
Imagine yourself lying on the bottom of a flowing riverbed looking upwards. You notice leaves and twigs floating past above you. Treat cravings or anxieties just like the leaves – you simply notice and observe them as they pass.

Noticing your thoughts and feelings each time you go to light up, helps you 'step back' from the habit of smoking. Now you have more influence over your addiction rather than your addiction having influence over you. Observing yourself is also a way of plugging back into your life and your life force, rather than life 'living' you.

Centring yourself makes it easier to part company with smoking when you decide to do so. In the meantime, you can say 'I am deciding to have a cigarette because ...', which is better than an automatic response to light up when the phone rings or you're about to have a drink.

ALTERNATIVES

As part of your preparation for thinking, feeling and behaving more objectively about smoking, write down three small things you're going to do instead of smoking. For example, 'Enjoy being with friends, without smoking, even if they do' or 'Talk on the phone with a glass of water to hand.' It doesn't matter how small your steps are – just beginning to feel differently towards smoking and expressing this in little manageable ways each day can help bring about change.

1. _____
2. _____
3. _____

'Our tears prepare the ground for our future growth',
Julia Cameron, *The Artist's Way* (Pan Books, 1995)

Make your fantasy a reality

Affirm you're already a non-smoker (whether you are or not, behave as if you are) by doing something each day to bring your fantasy into reality. For example, make your car or a room in your house a 'no-smoking' zone; put a single life-affirming flower in a vase or glass on a table as a reminder of your improving good health.

Make a note of your ideas here.

_____

_____

_____

_____

Focusing your thoughts

Recognize your fears as part of you, learn to notice them and embrace them. Try simply observing them ('Ah, there it is again') – but without judgement. It's perfectly OK to feel fearful – just keep centring and choose to embrace change.

'You can take a negative approach where you decide all change is disruptive and therefore bad; this will foster anxiety or even dread, which causes kidneys to contract, causing even more anxiety and dread. Or you can take a positive approach where change is good, which will trigger your adventuresome spirit, causing your pulse to quicken and your energy to flow more strongly', The Barefoot Doctor

SELF-COACHING TIPS
- *Fear can stop you from embracing change. Have confidence and faith.*
- *Repeat your affirmation as often as possible, then practise grounding. Do this – even for a few seconds each day – and feel the difference.*
- *Notice how disgusting a full ashtray looks when you empty it.*
- *Decide to commit every day to what you're doing.*
- *Keep encouraging yourself.*
- *Keep your attention on how you'd like things to be.*
- *Give yourself time – but don't lose momentum.*
- *Enjoy each step of your journey.*

Commitment scale

How committed are you, at this point in time, to continue preparing yourself for stopping smoking?

Rate yourself on a scale of 1 to 10, where 1 is no commitment and 10 is totally committed: 1 2 3 4 5 6 7 8 9 10

10 Step 4: Resolving doubts

'Instead of giving power to an obstacle or limitation, by trying to repress, ignore or destroy it, we can do the opposite – we can claim the power we have invested in the obstacle ... and dissolve it internally; by claiming it ... and digesting it ... we release ourselves from its limiting effects. We are then free to move on', Ken Mellor

So far you have learnt three primary ways to help you achieve your goal – and each builds on and supports the other:

1. Grounding. This allows you to live in the present moment, to relax, to concentrate and to communicate more effectively. It also allows you to dissolve negative emotions and to enhance good feelings.

2. Focusing on what you want to achieve in a way that helps you experience success. This is profoundly influenced by your own expectations of success.

3. Staying centred and keeping on track in a way that allows you to deal with cravings (or any anxiety) in a calm and serene way.

Time to clear mixed feelings

The fourth technique in your Toolkit for Success is, in some ways, the most valuable, because it helps deal with something very fundamental – so fundamental it's usually overlooked – and that is your ambivalence about quitting. Quitters are urged to simply 'keep on trying' or 'don't give up giving up', because the relapse rate is so high. But by using the following technique, around 75 per cent of my clients after a year – considerably higher than the national average of around 23–5 per cent – have managed to quit successfully.

'By its nature, anything that's repressed comes back again', Anon

Unhook yourself, release yourself

The technique you're about to learn is very effective in helping many smokers quit successfully. It enables you to identify – and deal with – a profound and common issue around quitting. This issue, if it is not resolved, may cause repeated relapses or keep you trapped in a cycle of 'trying to stop smoking'. What's the issue? It's that there is probably part of you that still wants to smoke.

The technique, 'unifying', is about helping you go back and 'unhook' yourself so you can walk free and attain your goal. You can see it as a release – a way of releasing yourself from nicotine and the habit of smoking – and as a way of restoring a sense of freedom and vitality in you.

'The psychological rule says that when an inner situation is not made conscious, it happens outside, as fate; that is to say, when the individual remains undivided and does not become conscious of his inner contradictions, the world must, perforce, act out the conflict and be torn into opposite halves', Carl Gustav Jung, *Symbols of Transformation* (Princeton, 1956)

Unifying differs from other techniques because its focus is *freedom* – freedom from fears that are often never adequately dealt with, therefore never properly resolved, that cause relapse time and again.

What are the advantages to you of smoking?

Many other books and methods focus on the disadvantages of smoking. But how many pause to look at the advantages? Can you gloss over this vital aspect of an addiction and a habit that you may have enjoyed for years, ignoring the very reasons that have sustained you all this time? Of course not. That's why you need to fully re-experience what you're letting go, what you're replacing.

The advantages of smoking might include relaxation, companionship and relief from boredom. By identifying these, you can recognize that's where you're hooked – 'snagged on a branch'. So it's important to:

1. identify what needs you associate with smoking;
2. learn how to accept them before releasing them.

When you have done this, you can move on more easily.

Willpower and quick-fix methods

'Research has shown than 97 per cent of attempts to give up using willpower alone will fail', Reuters, January 2004.

Some methods of stopping smoking are about fighting the addiction (the physical aspect) or habit (the psychological aspect) using 'willpower'. This immediately sets up internal conflicts. Quitters then think 'willpower' is the cause of their failure. The 'willpower-based' methods often inadvertently support the energy of conflict and simply intensify the struggle. The focus – and your energy – is on the struggle – not the ease of resolution. The unifying exercise helps resolve these inner conflicts.

You may have seen quick-fix methods advertised, such as 'Stop Smoking in One Hour'. Although 'alternative' methods undoubtedly work for some quitters, they don't deal with the deep psychological ambivalence and inner conflict that many smokers experience. Often, they simply repress the desire to smoke, and this can manifest itself in symptoms such as hunger, loss of concentration and sleep – and may be just a temporary solution.

Avoiding temptation

Ignoring the nagging desire to smoke by simply avoiding people or situations where you might be tempted, or keeping yourself desperately busy all the time, soon becomes impossible. The internal struggle involved can end up with the quitter resuming smoking – often within a short time.

These methods simply make smoking the enemy and create further conflict. Anything that keeps you fighting keeps you stuck. Even if you experience victory, where you've managed to fight or suppress your desire to smoke, it's likely to be temporary if it's rooted in battle.

With other stop-smoking techniques, effort is often needed to support and maintain 'willpower'. It's assumed all the quitter needs to do is 'want to stop smoking', but this does not help to resolve their terrible dilemma: their mixed feelings about stopping smoking. Smokers understand only too well how much of their energy is locked into this ambivalence; they are unable to free themselves from smoking because part of them doesn't want to stop. Making a firm decision about stopping is, therefore, impossible.

Being stuck or locked in a battle over quitting because of your mixed feelings can have its advantages. Perhaps smoking has been useful or functional in the past? This makes a perfect excuse for not stopping smoking. 'I can't stop', you might say – and this would be partly true, because your desire and energy to stop smoking are held in check by your desire and energy to keep smoking.

You have the power

You are capable of stopping smoking *yourself*. Handing over this important responsibility to someone else – like a hypnotherapist or an acupuncturist – externalizes the remedy for quitting in the same way that you externalize the power cigarettes have over you (for example, 'I can't relax without a cigarette').

When quitters discover the 'unifying' technique, they often seem relieved. Accepting your (possible) desire to smoke and learning effective ways of dealing with it is one of the keys to stopping smoking successfully. That way, you don't engage in a battle with smoking or try to impose your will on your addiction.

Embrace your addiction

Unifying will teach you that instead of fighting your addiction and your habit, you can acknowledge and embrace them in a way that liberates you. You will be in charge of smoking rather than smoking being in charge of you. You will be able to rewrite your life!

The unifying exercise helps release you from your inner struggle where your energy and vitality are sapped by these two seemingly intractable parts of you, each pulling and pushing against the other, causing you to feel stuck and unable to make a clear decision.

The technique offers a unique way of actively encouraging you to re-experience, or 'act out', this dilemma, the one that faces most smokers: why you continue to smoke and why you want to quit. If you've tried to quit before, was this dilemma an issue for you?

- Yes
- No
- Don't know

TWO PARTS IN TENSION

1. Bring both your hands together, fingers straight, place them in the middle of your chest – like you're praying.
2. Press your palms firmly together for a minute.
3. When the time is up, release the pressure.
4. Notice how much energy is taken up when two parts that are in tension come together.

Let's do the following exercise, to identify why you continue to smoke. If you've quit, you will understand your addiction better and this will help to fully 'unhook' or 'unsnag' you.

FOR AND AGAINST

Write a list of all the things you enjoy about smoking.

1. _____
2. _____
3. _____
4. _____
5. _____

Write a list of all the reasons you want to stop smoking.

1. _____
2. _____
3. _____
4. _____
5. _____

Now choose the most powerful reason from each list and note them below. These represent the two 'parts' of you and your smoking. For example, 'I really enjoy a cigarette' and 'I want to live healthily'. You'll use these shortly when you do the unifying exercise.

1. _____
2. _____

The blame game

When smokers remain 'split' about whether or not they really want to quit, they often project these feelings onto others. They blame their spouse, job or situation for their failure to quit successfully. And often themselves. Sometimes you need to identify and reclaim the part of you that you're projecting onto other people or situations. So instead of saying 'I'd like to stop smoking, but work is too stressful', 'My family couldn't stand it if I tried again', or 'I'm bound to fail', you'd say 'I'd like to stop smoking, but I'm not ready at the moment'. This is where the 'unifying' exercise also helps.

Jot down an instance where you've blamed someone or something for your failure to quit:

_____

_____

_____

TOOLKIT FOR SUCCESS EXERCISE 4: UNIFYING

'Whoever has parted from his source, longs to return to that state of union', Rumi, 13th-century poet and mystic

This exercise is designed to free you up and make quitting clearer and easier. There are a number of steps, so take your time over it.

STEP 1
Imagine everything has worked out perfectly.

STEP 2
Ground your experiences so your system digests what you're experiencing. Move around to help release thoughts and feelings.

STEP 3
Choose the part of you that doesn't want to quit and stay with that part. Really get into it: act it out as fully as you can. Go through the ritual of lighting up, or imagine doing so.
• Take that first deep drag.
• Feel the 'hit' at the back of your throat.
• Experience the feeling of enjoyment that floods through you.
• Enjoy how relaxed you now feel, smoking your cigarette.

STEP 4
Ground your experiences.

STEP 5

Now act out the part that does want to quit. Really get into the feelings.
- Breathe in deeply.
- Smile with confidence.
- Hear the praise of family and friends.
- Stride up hills without effort.
- Enjoy the taste of food.
- Feel more loving and closer to people.
- Enjoy your feeling of self-esteem and confidence. You can do anything now.

STEP 6

Ground again.

STEP 7

Imagine conversations between the two parts; what's being said? Act out whatever's going on, any tensions or fighting between them.

STEP 8

Ground.

STEP 9

See everything all perfectly worked out. You've stopped smoking! You're free!

STEP 10

Ground.

STEP 11

Behave in a way that affirms your ideal outcome.
- Run for the bus.
- Go for a brisk walk in the fresh air.
- Eat something delicious and really savour the taste.

TIPS FOR UNIFYING

• *Having established why you smoke, it's important to experience what happens when you 'act' out your mixed feelings in the exercise. Just be as relaxed as you can about doing this. Part of making any decision is to spend time with different aspects of it.*

• *Recognize that your ambivalent response to smoking arises out of you. Both parts of the dilemma are part of you; otherwise, you wouldn't be experiencing mixed feelings about quitting.*

• *You can free yourself from this state of unnatural disequilibrium and instead experience harmony, unity and vitality.*

How will I know I've resolved my mixed feelings?

Keep going with it until you feel clear, 'unhooked'. You'll know when you've resolved your mixed feelings because you'll be much surer and clearer about achieving your goal. You'll know you're unified within when you no longer experience the push and pull of wanting, then not wanting, to quit and when you are not sabotaging yourself any more.

SELF-COACHING TIPS

• *Unifying helps you release yourself from focusing all your energy on the struggle associated with willpower and doubts. At the same time, it's good to remember not to do the opposite and put all your energy into wanting to quit. Just allow elements to build and progress.*

• *Another dilemma quitters sometimes face is 'I care about myself' and 'I don't care about myself'. Use unifying to help resolve these two conflicting aspects.*

• *Feel great about getting this far. Completing the unifying exercise means a part of you does want to stop smoking. If you find yourself weighing up the pros and cons, repeat the unifying exercise until you're resolved.*

• *When you've resolved your conflict internally, it automatically follows it'll be resolved externally as well.*

• *Keep your eye on your goal – especially when you're stuck.*

Commitment scale

How committed are you, at this point in time, to continue preparing yourself for stopping smoking?

Rate yourself on a scale of 1 to 10, where 1 is no commitment and 10 is totally committed: 1 2 3 4 5 6 7 8 9 10

11 Step 5: Managing change

'To access any capacity, we need to stay aware of, and thereby connected to, who and what we are', Ken and Elizabeth Mellor

This final chapter in Part 2 will enable you to best choose how to 'access' your own 'capacity' and make the necessary changes to your life as easy and enjoyable as possible. We'll also include the final technique in your toolkit for success: relaxation.

A change of lifestyle

Stopping smoking does not only mean changing your habits, such as the way you relax, take time out for yourself and cope with stress, but it can also mean a profound change of lifestyle. Like passing your driving test, you will realize that you need to pay close attention to doing certain things until you are confident that you can do them automatically. And this can have a ripple effect on the rest of your life.

Life tastes better

Successful quitters often experience most things in life as being much better. They find themselves making all sorts of changes because they're more connected with their own aliveness.

- They feel much better about themselves (and therefore others).
- They taste and smell things better (and they smell better!).
- They feel happier and more contented.
- They have a lot more energy and are more relaxed.

When you stop smoking, you will want to enhance these feelings and build on and enjoy your self-esteem, rediscovering simple sensual pleasures like tasting food and smelling flowers, exercising regularly and enjoying it.

What changes in your lifestyle would stopping smoking bring about?

_____

_____

IN TUNE WITH YOUR BODY

'Healing comes from slow inner evolution up to a point where a sudden dramatic change occurs, like the ripening of fruit, which painlessly and spontaneously falls when the time comes',
Professor Robert Molimard, Co-ordinator of DIU Tobacologie Paris
(GLOBALink, May 2006)

The way we experience life is through our bodies. Life tastes better, and is easier, when you are:
• in tune with your physical body;
• alert to the many cues that come from your physical system;
• physically aware of how you respond to yourself;
• as healthy and physically active as you can be;
• responding to physical needs in an attentive way.
As a smoker, do you tend to listen to the messages your body gives you – like hunger, tiredness, loneliness, boredom?
• Yes
• No
Do you tend to use cigarettes as a way of dealing with these 'messages'?
• Yes
• No
As a smoker do you think you interact with, and respond to, your body differently from non-smokers?
• Yes
• No
If 'Yes', how? If 'No', say why.

_____
_____
_____
_____

How are you going to manage things differently when you quit?

_____
_____
_____
_____

How often is, or was, the effect of the cigarette a way of meeting some need in you – like dealing with stress?
• Often
• Occasionally
• Hardly at all

Healing stress

Stress now accounts for over 70 per cent of visits to the doctor and is one of the most common reasons for taking time off work. Stress also creates high adrenaline levels. Adrenaline stays in the bloodstream for about 18 hours, so if you're regularly stressed – as smokers often are – you're flooding your body almost continuously with large quantities of this chemical. There are several effective ways of reducing adrenaline and stress levels:
• Focus on your breathing (see the exercise below).
• Physical exercise (this is the most effective way, so decide what kind you'll choose: brisk walking, swimming, a workout).
• Grounding (to help deal with any intense feelings; see page 60)
• Centring (to enable you to stay calm; see page 81).

The following exercises are great ways to help you relax. Get into the habit of repeating them as often as you can, you'll find they calm and rejuvenate you and allow you to create new habits. The more you repeat them, the greater your enjoyment and benefit and the better your connection with your own, nourishing life force. And you can do them anywhere, any time – they are completely private.

BE MINDFUL OF YOUR BREATHING

Deliberately focusing on your breathing brings you into the present moment. Whenever you experience cravings, distract yourself from them by turning your attention to your breath. Close your eyes and focus on your breathing – just observe it. Practise and experiment with this exercise so that it's automatically available to you.

REFLECT ON YOUR 'SPIRITUAL SIDE'

1. Sit quietly.
2. Close your eyes, breathe in and out deeply a few times.
3. Connect with peace for a few seconds.

Jot down your experience:

_____
_____
_____
_____

MEDITATION

1. Sit upright on a chair or cross-legged on the floor with a straight back.
2. Make sure you're comfortable.
3. Close your eyes and breathe in and out deeply a few times.
4. Focus your awareness in the point between your eyebrows.
5. If thoughts come into your mind, acknowledge them and let them drift away like clouds and then resume your focus.
6. Do this for a few minutes each day and see what happens.

Choose some situations to use breathing as a calming way or a way to distract yourself. Make a note of them here.

_____
_____
_____
_____

TOOLKIT FOR SUCCESS EXERCISE 5: RELAXATION

This final tool aims to anchor the mind in the moment and turn off what Buddhists refer to as the 'monkey mind', the chattering mind. You can breathe away your anxieties, which will help you to quit more easily. Relaxation is natural; your body relaxes automatically and easily when allowed to do so, but habits like smoking interfere with this. Use relaxation techniques instead of cigarettes:

• to help you unwind;
• to release feelings and tensions in stressful situations;
• to increase pleasure and ease;
• to increase the effectiveness of your affirmations;
• to help with sleep (your sleep patterns can be affected by quitting);
• to contribute significantly to your own healing.

STEP 1

Kneel, or sit if this is easier, in a relaxed but alert posture.

STEP 2

Close your eyes.

STEP 3

Notice the contact your body is making with whatever is supporting you.

STEP 4

Become aware of your breathing. With each out-breath you become a little more relaxed.

STEP 5

Breathe deeply. Concentrate on the movement of air in and out of your body.

STEP 6

Imagine any tensions draining away from your head, down through your body and out through your feet leaving you feeling calm and relaxed.

STEP 7

Repeat and note any differences in how you feel.

Each time you breathe out, you'll see yourself becoming clearer, more transparent, quieter and stiller, more harmonious. You will feel slacker, looser. You will look clearer, brighter, taste sweeter. You will smell more fragrant.

YOUR PLACE IN THE WORLD

**'The unfolding of our connection to something greater than ourselves is the essential element necessary for our profound healing',
N. Wellings and E. McCormick**

Do you want to connect better and more fully with yourself and others?
• Yes
• No
• Don't know

Do you think our relationships to ourselves and others is the means by which we really know ourselves and discover our place in the world?
• Yes
• No
• Don't know

Do you think one way to help you better achieve this is by stopping smoking?
• Yes
• No
• Don't know

EXPERIENCE VERSUS BELIEF

It's important for your sake that you don't simply believe what I'm saying but that you trust your own experience and experiment for yourself to find out what works for you.

Do you see this whole experience as a healing relationship with yourself?
• Yes
• No

List three ways in which you've decided to manage yourself – and your everyday life – differently.

1. _____
2. _____
3. _____

'If the best of all possible worlds were reality, most of us would do things a little differently. We can begin to make the best a reality by doing things a little differently now', Julia Cameron, *The Sound of Paper* (Michael Joseph, 2004)

SELF-COACHING TIPS
• *When reading the list overleaf, note that the benefits start straight away.*
• *See any withdrawal symptoms that you may experience as part of the healing process.*
• *Circle any facts that really grab you – use these in your imagination and visualizations to bring about a healthy you.*

How the body repairs itself after quitting *

TIME SINCE QUITTING

20 minutes
• blood pressure and pulse rate return to normal

1 hour
• circulation improves
• hands and feet feel warmer

2 hours
• improved blood supply to skin

8 hours
• nicotine and carbon monoxide levels in blood fall
• oxygen in your blood increases and is returning to normal

24 hours
• carbon monoxide completely eliminated from body
• lungs start to clear out the mucous and other smoking debris

48 hours
• virtually no nicotine left in the bloodstream
• sense of taste and smell improves

72 hours
• breathing becomes easier
• bronchial tubes begin to relax
• energy levels increase

1–2 weeks
• withdrawal symptoms ease

2–3 weeks
• physical withdrawal symptoms have stopped
• risk of blood clots reduced

• breathing and energy levels continue to improve

2–12 weeks
• circulation to hands and feet improves
• skin looks fresher
• overall energy levels increase

3–9 months
• coughs, wheezing and breathing problems should disappear as lungs are better able to resist infection

1 year
• risk of cancer of mouth and throat is half that of a smoker
• risk of developing cardiovascular disease is haved

5 years
• risk of throat, oesophageal and bladder cancer is halved

5–10 years
• risk of developing cardiovascular disease or blood clots is the same as for a non-smoker

10 years
• risk of lung cancer falls to half that of a smoker
• risk of developing osteoporosis decreases

10–15 years
• risk of lung, throat, oesophageal or bladder cancer is the same as for a non-smoker

* based on 1990 US Surgeon's Report

HOW DO YOU FEEL?

As a result of reading the list, do you appreciate the following?
How much smoking affects your entire system?
- Yes
- No

How quickly the body responds when it's given the opportunity to get back into natural balance?
- Yes
- No

How amazing it is that this return to equilibrium happens in a relatively short time, given the length of time you may have been smoking?
- Yes
- No

How empowering it is to make such profound changes to your health by quitting?
- Yes
- No

Alternatively, are you still weighing up the pros and cons of quitting?
- Yes
- No

Are you worrying about how you'll cope with some possible discomfort for a short while?
- Yes
- No

Are you worrying about the prospect of leaving your 'comfort zone'?
- Yes
- No

Change can mean loss

If smoking is a way of life for you, then not smoking might feel like a loss. You might experience it as a loss of structure, of pleasure, of a way of communicating, of a way of life. Although you may find quitting relatively 'easy', you will need to make adjustments.

Change usually involves some level of discomfort, and whenever you stop doing something you've been doing for a while, there's some degree of loss.

- Take care of yourself.
- Nurture yourself.
- Be patient.
- Use the Toolkit for Success to help you deal with any challenges.
- Quitters often find that creating a new habit – for example, a physical activity – in place of smoking helps them to cope with the change as well as providing a practical and useful alternative.

Change can take time

Change doesn't always happen overnight. The Toolkit for Success is not a 'miracle' or instant cure. A lot of issues that arise for you will probably have taken place over a long period and may need time and effort on your part to resolve. It's important not to force any solutions but continue to take small steps, just like you're doing.

YOUR WINDOW OF OPPORTUNITY

A change is occurring within you, which may, or may not, be clear to you. But consciously or unconsciously you're giving yourself an opportunity to make the changes you know, deep down, you want to make. Otherwise this wouldn't be happening to you.

Remind yourself of the main reason why you want to quit smoking.

_____
_____
_____
_____

How has this 'change' occurred?

_____
_____
_____
_____

How involved has your body been in this process?

_____
_____
_____
_____

Does it seem as if your body has presented you with a 'window of opportunity' that you're now listening to?

_____

_____

_____

_____

Acknowledge the change – however subtle it may seem – and decide to do something different from the usual pattern of 'lighting up'.

Start 'observing' yourself

See this change, however gradual, as a great step forward. Instead of getting twitchy, angry or aggressive when you want a cigarette, start the process of 'separating' yourself from your habit – 'observing yourself'. Simply pause for a few seconds and ask yourself 'what's this about?' or 'what do I really want or need?'

• Tune into your body to find out what's going on for you.
• Centre yourself.
• Ground yourself.
• Keep repeating this. Each time you repeat the grounding, you'll experience a shift. You'll be better able to recognize and respond to your needs and alternative ways of behaving than simply lighting up.

You already know how to make changes

Remember you're embarking on something that's also familiar to you: you already know how to make changes in your life – including things you've created in the past but then decided you don't like. You also know how to change behaviour that requires you to stop doing something.

Remember, you've already been a non-smoker – even though it was a long time ago. Returning to live your life without cigarettes means you're reviving something that's already there – a bit like taking up playing the piano, swimming or riding a bike years after first learning how. You already know what this is like – and that it's possible.

'GIVE IT UP'

What are you really 'giving up'? Smoking – and thinking about smoking – is probably with you from morning until night, depending on your habit.

As a moderate to heavy smoker, smoking is pretty much always on your mind; it's part of your identity and can affect your whole lifestyle.
Make a list of five things you might find hard to 'give up'.

1. _____
2. _____
3. _____
4. _____
5. _____

Make a list of five things you are looking forward to 'giving up'.

1. _____
2. _____
3. _____
4. _____
5. _____

Now look at your life and list three situations that are influenced by your smoking – and, as a non-smoker, you wouldn't need to do. This list could include:

• having to go outside to smoke;
• the disapproval of your partner, children, family, friends and doctor;
• your spending more time with friends who smoke;
• going to particular pubs or cafés where you can smoke;
• being more likely to befriend colleagues who smoke;
• being attracted to jobs that have smoke breaks.

1. _____
2. _____
3. _____

Rebels without a cause

You may think or believe that smoking singles you out as an individual, a rebel, an interesting person, that it makes you look cool or more sexy. Or maybe this image is becoming a bit out of date and possibly foolish, especially when you're forced to smoke outdoors at work, often huddled together in all weathers with your fellow smokers.

**' "All the most amusing people" are the ones bravely courting bronchitis, emphysema, heart disease and cancer out in the garden',
Catherine Bennett (the *Guardian*, January 2001)**

The 'dry alcoholic' and the 'ex-smoker'

Have you heard the term 'dry alcoholic'? It forms part of a popular belief system that states 'once an alcoholic, always an alcoholic'. So many ex-alcoholics believe and accept this is true. But while it might help them stop drinking, the phrase 'dry alcoholic' doesn't help them deal with their dependency issues ('I'll always be an alcoholic'). It can be the same for quitters: 'once a smoker, always a smoker'.

You'll find the toolkit offers you an opportunity for change at a much deeper level, helping you deal with core problems around smoking and quitting, not just a 'symptom' change where you stop smoking and remain an 'ex-smoker' for ever. The toolkit is also beneficial for those who've quit, to help deal with any underlying issues that may be unresolved – and therefore help you stay stopped for good.

FIVE SCENARIOS

To help you understand your dependency as fully as possible, so you can successfully manage change and avoid or deal with relapse, jot down five different scenarios you think you might experience when you're in the early stages of quitting. For example, 'I'm really worried it's going to be difficult' or 'I know I get really anxious when I'm socializing'. Just jot down what comes into your mind.

1. _____
2. _____
3. _____
4. _____
5. _____

Five of the most frequent scenarios that arise are:

1. How am I going to cope if there's a problem?
2. I'm worried I'll fail (again).
3. I'm still not sure if I really want to stop.
4. I know it's going to be hard.
5. I really enjoy a cigarette, it helps me relax.

How do these compare with the ones on your list?

• Similar
• Not similar

A TECHNIQUE FOR EACH SCENARIO

These five scenarios tend to be among the most common anxieties. They provide a template to help you identify, as easily as possible, the most suitable 'tool' from your toolkit for success to manage change differently. Each scenario corresponds to the five tools listed below:

1. Grounding, to help keep you balanced and living in the present moment, so you're not worrying or anxious.

2. Centring, to help you 'observe' your behaviour in a calm and serene manner.

3. Unifying, to help resolve doubts.

4. Creating What you Want for Yourself, to help visualize your own success.

5. Relaxation, to help you tap into your own, natural ability to relax.

Decide from the toolkit which exercises you're 'drawn to' as a way of helping you manage change differently. This might be all of them at different times, depending on the situation. Repeat each scenario from your list above, and then note which tool you can use for each one.

1. _____

TOOL: _____

2. _____

TOOL: _____

3. _____

TOOL: _____

4. _____

TOOL: _____

5. _____

TOOL: _____

You've already made changes

'Leap and the net will appear', Julia Cameron, *The Artist's Way*

Although the idea of change can be alarming, remember all the changes you've already made in your life – particularly the big ones: deciding to leave your job and start another one, moving house, getting married, having children, getting divorced.

Maybe you felt the same way then as you do now, wondering how you'll manage the changes, whether you've made the right decision, fearful of being without those familiar comforts and taking a plunge into the unknown.

YOUR LIFE CHANGES

Think of your life in terms of the changes you've already made. Note down three big changes:

1. _____

2. _____

3. _____

Looking back, what personal strengths and resources did you draw on to help you?

_____

_____

_____

_____

Did you get any help for yourself?

_____

_____

_____

_____

If not, looking back, do you wish you had got help?

• Yes

• No

Why was this?

_____

_____

_____

_____

What qualities did you bring to the situation that helped you make the change?

_____

_____

_____

_____

Was there a time when you thought it wasn't going to be OK?

_____

_____

_____

_____

If so, what kept you going?

_____

_____

_____

_____

Although it might have been difficult, are you glad you went through with it?
• Yes
• No

These big changes are also big achievements, regardless of how well you think you accomplished them. So when you think of managing the changes you might make to your health and lifestyle by stopping smoking, allow yourself the pleasure of knowing you can achieve things – however challenging they might seem at the time.

Every minute counts

Are you willing to use your spare time as a way of further committing yourself to managing change differently?
• Yes
• No

Time is available to you while you're on public transport, at traffic lights, walking, swimming and gardening. Welcome this as time, it allows you to do the following:
• Breathing exercises.
• Techniques from the Toolkit for Success.
• Take a few deep breaths instead of lighting up.
• Cope with stress by relaxing and grounding.

- Change your mindset so you do things differently.
- Be more connected with your physical body.
- Experiment with other ways of coping.

Focusing your thoughts

Remember, start in the same way you mean to finish. Once you've committed yourself to making the decision to quit, behave in a way that is consistent with achieving your goal – as if you've already achieved it.

SELF-COACHING TIPS

- *Remind yourself how much you've already achieved. Call on memories of past successes; they are powerful reminders that you can succeed.*
- *Remind yourself regularly what you're good at. Write down every quality and achievement you're proud of.*

_____

_____

_____

_____

- *Changing deep-rooted patterns in your life by changing the behaviour associated with them takes courage, faith, commitment and compassion. So congratulate yourself.*

'The old skin has to be shed before the new one can come', Joseph Campbell

Commitment scale

How committed are you, at this point in time, to continue preparing yourself for stopping smoking?

Rate yourself on a scale of 1 to 10, where 1 is no commitment and 10 is totally committed: 1 2 3 4 5 6 7 8 9 10

PART 3: ACTION

12 Introduction to the sessions

'Look at every path closely and deliberately. Try it as many times as you think necessary. Then ask yourself and yourself alone one question … Does this path have heart? If it does, the path is good. If it doesn't, it is of no use', Carlos Castenada, *The Teachings of Don Juan* (Penguin, 1968)

Congratulations on completing Parts 1 and 2 of the book. Each part supports and connects with the others, helping you make a mental and emotional 'shift' in your attitude to smoking and what it does for you – and to you. Part 2 offers a proven toolkit of techniques to help you deal with a range of likely situations, such as temptation, stress, social situations or self-doubt.

The five sessions in Part 3 give you the opportunity to put the techniques learnt in Part 2 into practice, in a focused and manageable way, to consolidate what you've learnt so far to help maximize your chances of success.

Your menu

Think of the sessions and the toolkit as a 'menu' from which you can choose the best option to suit each occasion. You'll find some overlap with Parts 1 and 2 here. This means you can complete each session more easily – as the parts relate to and build on each other. For example, the grounding technique really supports both the visualization exercise, 'Creating What You Want For Yourself' and the centring technique. You can repeat sessions as often as you need in order to master the techniques before moving on.

Take your time

Remember, the high relapse rate is largely due to quitters moving on too quickly and not resolving their fears and doubts. Simply having the desire to quit is often not enough. You also need to know how to bring this desire about.

We learn through repetition, so sometimes we need to keep taking ourselves back to situations in order to resolve them. If you experience a slip-up after you set your quit date – say, by putting yourself in a vulnerable position by going to the pub before you're ready, then you know you need to repeat a particular session and deal with that issue.

Each session relates to a toolkit technique or 'step' in Part 2. So think of these as actual steps – ones you can go up and down as much as you need, and in your own time, in order to progress. Repeating sessions – or steps – is also progress.

Who can use the sessions?

The skills you develop here will help with most difficulties or challenges in your life, as well as enabling you to enjoy and enhance your life as fully as possible, too. Who will benefit from the sessions?

• Individuals who want to quit – either by themselves, with a friend, family member or 'buddy'.
• Smokers who need further motivation, inspiration or assurance before committing themselves to quitting.
• Quitters who've already stopped smoking and are looking for ongoing support in order to prevent relapse.
• Health professionals in the field – including health promotion workers and those in primary care.
• Clinicians and health counsellors in the private sector or those working in a health or workplace setting.

What's involved?

The sessions focus in a practical way on several main areas:
• Core themes for quitters: what drives old habits?
• What are the issues that smokers and quitters need to look at?
• What causes relapse?
• What are the tools and techniques you need to help you quit successfully and stay quit?

Setting a quit date

Each session has its own theme, including natural ways to beat stress, encourage self-motivation, deal with any fears and focus on commitment as a means of furthering your goal. The whole programme is designed so you focus on the ease of quitting.

The session in which you set your quit date happens to be Session 4. This is based on the number of sessions it usually takes for quitters to feel ready to do so. But it's up to you. The important thing is to set a quit date when you feel ready, when you've mastered the techniques sufficiently to feel confident – maybe even excited – about parting company with cigarettes.

The sessions are designed to help you look forward to quitting by enabling you to:

• find or clarify your own personal reason for doing so;

• learn how to create your success and stay focused on your goal;

• use the skills, practical tips, techniques and exercises in the book to help deal with any fears and doubts and to let go of old patterns;

• realize the importance of taking responsibility for your own actions;

• decide to commit yourself to furthering your goal by doing something enjoyable every day to promote it – including looking after yourself in various ways, such as physical exercise and healthy eating.

If you've quit already, the sessions will help you stay stopped successfully.

The principles

A lot of material in these sessions is unique in the field of smoking cessation and is based on several fundamental principles:

• Your body is an immense source of natural power and resources which you can learn to tap into at any time.

• You can connect with your life force so you're more in touch with your own happiness and aliveness.

• You can get to know your body by listening to fears and doubts and responding in particular ways to bring about your success.

• You can influence and alter your mindset to completely change the way you think about what cigarettes do for you.

• You can free yourself from feeling trapped or stuck around smoking – or any other difficulty.

Skills for life

The principles used here are the same ones I use in life coaching. So the skills you develop here will help with other difficulties and challenges in your life, beyond smoking. These might include dealing with stress at work, difficulties between you and others, helping you to be clear about your goals. These techniques are also a great means of enabling you to live more mindfully, creatively and peacefully, and to enjoy and enhance your life as much as possible.

13

Session 1: Connecting to your life force

'Once the connection is made with your true (underlying) self, as opposed to the self you present to the world... you will instantaneously feel reconnected to the rest of creation', **Barefoot Doctor**

At this stage you'll have familiarized yourself with the five techniques in Part 2 and may be at the point of change, where you are committed to quitting. Now we'll focus more on putting these skills into everyday practice. This first session is linked with the first technique (or 'toolkit exercise') in Part 2, the second session with the second 'tool' and so on, so you'll be developing and expanding on your skills in a practical, focused way. As part of this process, you'll continue to rate yourself using the scale at the end of each session to assess your commitment to quitting.

What's involved in this session?

AIMS
• To help you get further in touch with your own inner capacity to restore calm and health in your life.
• To help deal with everyday situations and challenges, like stress or socializing.
• To help deal with feelings stopping smoking may stimulate in you.

WE WILL COVER
• Your reasons and triggers for smoking.
• Your body as the main source of help.
• Living in the present.
• Managing positive and negative feelings.

- How attitudes affect us.
- Learning the secret of contentment and well-being.
- What's in a cigarette?

TECHNIQUE: GROUNDING
SELF-COACHING TIPS
EXERCISES

Lighting up

Let's look at your reasons for lighting up. Do you usually smoke to deal with stress, to relax?
- Yes
- No

What are your automatic 'triggers' (for example a cup of tea or coffee, after a meal, driving)?

_____

_____

_____

_____

What was the reason for lighting up your last cigarette?

_____

_____

_____

_____

Recognizing how often worry or anxiety is a trigger for you is a better way of dealing with feelings than automatically lighting up. Next time you feel like a cigarette, just be aware of what's going on inside your body. For example are you feeling empty, anxious or happy? 'Observing' yourself in this way will help you quit more easily when you're ready.

Your own natural powerhouse

How you think largely determines the way you feel. And vice versa, the way you feel can also influence your whole being and approach to life. Your entire body – including your thoughts, feelings and behaviour

– is available to you to help you stop smoking successfully, without the need to resort to NRT. A positive frame of mind can help you succeed in almost every aspect of your life. (We'll deal more fully with this in the next session.)

There's increasing evidence to demonstrate that our attitudes – the way we think, feel and act – affect the way our bodies function and even the structure of our brains. Changing your attitude to smoking can actually change the structure of your brain. When you begin to think and feel differently about yourself and smoking, you make a major contribution to your health. Focusing on success as often as possible is very likely to help you and, conversely, focusing on failure is very likely *not* to help you.

Remember, our bodies work best when we're aware of our physical selves as well as our physical surroundings – in other words, well-grounded. When we're in a natural state of connectedness we 'instantaneously feel reconnected to the rest of creation'. Smoking tends to interrupt this natural process: smokers often feel constricted, closed down and unconnected. Many say they use cigarettes to help them feel better, and there's a lot of research to support the view that many smokers are depressed.

Living in the here and now

Learning to live in the here and now will help deal with these situations more easily. You can use it to enhance good feelings as well – in any area of your life. The grounding technique (described in full on page 60) is a great way to dissolve any inner obstacles you might have reconnecting with your 'true' self – as opposed to the one you usually connect and relate to the world with. This is the part of you that operates largely from your 'outer edge' as opposed to your 'inner core'.

Smokers who've learnt grounding say some of the effects are similar to smoking, without any of the harmful effects:
• instant feelings of peacefulness and warmth throughout your body;
• a feeling of 'connectedness';
• alertness and 'aliveness';
• release of worries and tension – to the point of not being bothered by whatever was troubling you;
• a sense of vitality.

A far healthier alternative

Well-grounded people tend to manage their feelings more easily, think more clearly and embrace change in a more relaxed way. 'Grounding' is a powerful exercise that helps you in the following ways:

• It frees you from worries and brings you into the present moment.
• It spreads calm and balance throughout your body.
• It brings you into the here and now.
• It regenerates and restores a natural equilibrium.
• It provides a healthy alternative to smoking.
• It can help manage the way you think, feel and act towards yourself in relation to smoking – or anything else for that matter.
• Repeat the grounding exercise for a few seconds as often as you can, especially when you're aware of a craving from your body.

TIME TO REFLECT

Stopping smoking is not a single, magical act. Most quitters don't simply wake up one morning and suddenly decide they want to quit and manage to do that successfully. It's usually a process they go through, one which can often be triggered by a single event, a 'signal' or 'turning point' – even for smokers who had no real intention to quit.

Think about your own position. Did you have a health scare? Was a particular birthday coming up? Did you want to get pregnant? Or did you simply become aware of a desire that surfaced, suddenly or slowly, nudging you to change your lifestyle?

What 'signs' or signals have you experienced that are affecting, or have affected, your desire to stop smoking?

_____

_____

_____

_____

What are your thoughts and feelings about stopping smoking?

_____

_____

_____

_____

Have they changed over time?
- Yes
- No

Have they changed gradually/suddenly?
- Yes
- No

In what way have they changed?

_____

_____

_____

_____

FACE YOUR NEGATIVE FEELINGS

When you think about the absence of cigarettes in your life what are you experiencing? Be as negative and panicky as you want.

_____

_____

_____

_____

Rate your level of anxiety on a scale of 1 to 10 where 1 is feeling very negative and 10 is very positive
1 2 3 4 5 6 7 8 9 10

Practise grounding to take care of any feelings that have been stirred up in you, to bring you back into balance and equilibrium. You can also practise grounding when you're thinking about lighting up. Pause, even if it's just for a few seconds, and do the exercise, then see whether you still really want the cigarette. A lot of quitters find they no longer do. Experiment for yourself.

Turn the negative into positive

Another tip if you experience negative thoughts or feelings when you think about quitting is to use these feelings to trigger the exact opposite: to remind you of what you do want, for example turn 'I don't think I'll succeed' to 'I do think I'll succeed'. Then go to your body to ground or digest the feelings to bring you back into balance.

WHAT ARE YOU FEELING?

The next time you light up, ask yourself these questions:

• What need in me is this cigarette fulfilling?

_____

_____

_____

_____

• What feelings am I experiencing when I go to light up? (Am I bored, angry, happy, sad?)

_____

_____

_____

_____

• What is the cigarette helping me cope with?

_____

_____

_____

_____

When you've finished note your comments about what you were feeling when you reached for a cigarette.

_____

_____

_____

_____

Is there a pattern? For example, are you lonely or bored in the evening?
• Yes
• No

List alternative activities to counter these feelings. (For example, if you feel lonely, you could ring a friend).

_____

_____

_____

Everyday grounding

Practise 'grounding' in certain places or situations:
- every time you sit down
- washing the dishes
- waiting at traffic lights.

Repeating this exercise will help you achieve your goal more easily: the more you practise it, the easier and quicker you can do it and get results.

TWO-DAY SMOKER'S DIARY

Complete the two-day diary, concentrating on the question 'What are you feeling when you go to light up?'

TIME	What are you doing?	Who are you with?	What are you feeling?	Did you enjoy it?

TIME	What are you doing?	Who are you with?	What are you feeling?	Did you enjoy it?

IDENTIFY YOUR ATTITUDE

This exercise will help you look at your attitude to your addiction and why you smoke. Knowing your own personal thoughts, feelings and behaviour will make it easier for you to quit. Fill in the answers at the end of the day.

DAY 1

Did you start off feeling positive today?
• Yes
• No
Did you find you needed a cigarette to help kick start?
• Yes
• No
Did you find you needed a cigarette to feel 'happier'?
• Yes
• No
Did you find you needed a cigarette to feel more 'alive?'
• Yes
• No

Assuming something went wrong, did you reach for a cigarette to help you deal with it?
- Yes
- No

Were you honest with others about how you were feeling – without having to resort to a cigarette?
- Yes
- No

If you needed a break – or to reward yourself – did you reach for a cigarette?
- Yes
- No

If you needed to relax, did you reach for a cigarette?
- Yes
- No

If you felt unhappy, did you reach for a cigarette?
- Yes
- No

What did you do today to promote your own happiness that didn't involve smoking?

_____
_____
_____
_____

DAY 2

Did you start off feeling positive today?
- Yes
- No

Did you find you needed a cigarette to help kick start?
- Yes
- No

Did you find you needed a cigarette to feel 'happier'?
- Yes
- No

Did you find you needed a cigarette to feel more 'alive?'
- Yes

- No

Assuming something went wrong, did you reach for a cigarette to help you deal with it?
- Yes
- No

Were you honest with others about how you were feeling – without having to resort to a cigarette?
- Yes
- No

If you needed a break – or to reward yourself – did you reach for a cigarette?
- Yes
- No

If you needed to relax, did you reach for a cigarette?
- Yes
- No

If you felt unhappy, did you reach for a cigarette?
- Yes
- No

What did you do today to promote your own happiness that didn't involve smoking?

_____
_____
_____
_____

If you answered mostly 'Yes' for Days 1 and 2, what are you doing to change this?

_____
_____
_____
_____

'Our sensations, feelings, thoughts and expectations are influenced by our bodies. So take over that influence and guide it, so it helps and supports your health and well-being, rather than hindering them', Ken and Elizabeth Mellor

WHAT'S IN A CIGARETTE?

Notice what you're feeling when you read the list below. Circle those that most affect you.

Write down your reaction after reading the list.

Substance	Found in
Acetone	nail varnish remover
Acetic acid	vinegar
Ammonia	anti-personnel spray, cleaning agent
Arsenic	ant poison in the USA
Benzene	petrol fumes
Cadmium	batteries, smelting fumes
Carbon monoxide	exhaust fumes
Carbon tetrachloride	dry cleaning fluid
DDT	insecticide
Formaldehyde	embalming fluid
Hydrocarbons	Jeyes fluid, car care agents
Hydrogen cyanide	industrial pollutant used in executions in USA
Hydrogen sulphide	stink bombs
Lead	batteries, petrol fumes
Methanol	rocket fuel
Methyl isocyanate	poison responsible for Bhopal disaster
Nicotine	insecticide
Nitric acid	power-station emissions
Polonium 210	radioactive fallout
Radon	radioactive gas
Sulphuric acid	power-station emissions
Tars	road surface tar
Toluene	industrial solvent

_____

_____

_____

_____

What action are you taking at the moment?

_____

_____

_____

_____

ACTIVE COMMITMENT

Choose an activity you like doing – such as walking, meditating, yoga, gardening, cycling, swimming.

Associate it with a way of affirming your goal.

Commit to doing it every day – and enjoying it.

You can change the activity whenever you want – the key is to anchor enjoying the activity with freedom from smoking.

SELF-COACHING TIPS

• _Our systems are stirred up and activated by new ideas and new goals; we're challenged to take notice of them. Grounding is a great way to help manage and release intense feelings._

• _Take small, manageable steps. When you think about your habit, be aware of changes you've already made (such as picking up this book or wishing you didn't smoke). Small steps or gradual changes can lead to larger ones._

• _Making any decision as easy as possible includes giving yourself time and space; balance this with keeping up the momentum of your desire to quit._

• _You needn't be at the mercy of your feelings. Remember that 'Our sensations, feelings, thoughts and expectations are influenced by our bodies. So take over that influence and guide it, so it helps and supports your health and well-being, rather than hindering them'._

• _Get into the habit of noticing your physical experiences._

• _When the body is overloaded with stimulation, we tend to feel angry (and more likely to light up). When it's balanced and at ease, we tend to feel content, happy or comfortable._

Commitment scale

How important is it to you that you stop smoking?

1 2 3 4 5 6 7 8 9 10

How committed are you to setting a quit date?

1 2 3 4 5 6 7 8 9 10

14

Session 2: Creating what you want for yourself

'For the caged bird sings of Freedom', Maya Angelou, *I Know Why the Caged Bird Sings* (Virago, 1993)

What's involved in this session?

AIMS
- Be clear about your goal and how to achieve it as easily as possible.
- Feel confident.
- Form new habits and ways of getting the things you want.
- Learn how to expect success.
- Maintain your goal.

WE WILL COVER
- Self-fulfilling prophecies.
- Changing unhelpful beliefs.
- How to achieve success.
- The importance of attitude.
- Dealing with self-doubt.
- Dealing with temptation.
- Maximizing success.

TECHNIQUE: VISUALIZATION
SELF-COACHING TIPS
EXERCISES

SELF-FULFILLING PROPHECIES

Most smokers spend a lot of time dwelling on negative thoughts, feelings and opinions when faced with challenges. They imagine that they will fail or that the successful quitters they know are 'better' or 'stronger' than they are. You can realize the power of your own expectations. Your success or failure rests largely with you. 'Self-fulfilling prophecies' can work for you or against you depending on your attitude.

Bearing in mind 'what you concentrate on is what you get', let's look at three questions:

1. What do you want to achieve?

_____
_____
_____
_____

2. Why do you want to achieve it?

_____
_____
_____
_____

3. How do you expect to achieve it? (Do you think it will be fairly easy, easy, difficult but you'll get there in the end, etc.)

_____
_____
_____
_____

If you want to run a new programme, remind yourself of what your old programme is:

How many cigarettes do you smoke daily?

_____
_____
_____
_____

At what age did you start smoking?

_____
_____
_____
_____

How many years have you been smoking?

_____

_____

_____

_____

Has this amount been fairly constant over the years – or has it gradually increased?

_____

_____

_____

_____

Have you tried to quit before?

_____

_____

_____

_____

How much do you spend on cigarettes each week?

_____

_____

_____

_____

How much will you save when you stop?

_____

_____

_____

_____

What's your attitude at the moment regarding quitting?
• Not quite ready yet.
• Thinking about it.
• Preparing to stop.
• Ready to set a quit date.
• Have already quit.

Change unhelpful beliefs

How can you achieve your goal as easily as possible? Did you know if you change the thoughts you programme into your brain, you can change the physical outcomes? Research supports this: if you believe something will happen and expect to benefit from it, this brings about changes in the body – even before it has happened. This session will provide you with the tools and skills to help channel your thoughts and feelings into positive behaviour that benefits you.

How you think largely determines the way you feel. Dopamine networks are triggered when we expect something 'good', whether that is food, sex or cigarettes – and actually change the systems in your brain and the chemical pathways that are 'wired together' when we form habits. Changing the association between smoking and pleasure helps break the cycle by changing the pathways. This is really exciting news because it means you can play an active part in your own healing.

YOU GET WHAT YOU EXPECT IN LIFE

If you expect to succeed, you generally do; if you expect to fail, you generally do. Likewise, if you expect that things will be difficult but that you'll get there in the end, this is likely to happen too.

Do you generally have the things you want in life, such as health, happiness, a good relationship, a job you enjoy?

_____

_____

_____

_____

Is there a direct relationship between getting what you want and getting what you expect?

_____

_____

_____

_____

Think of an area of your life where you expect to succeed, like every time you get into your car and expect you can drive.

Think about how often your expectations are fulfilled.

Now look at past attempts to quit (if you have attempted this in the past).

What was the biggest obstacle to your success?

_____

_____

_____

_____

How is it difficult this time?

_____

_____

_____

_____

How does that make you feel?

_____

_____

_____

_____

The golden keys to success

1. Developing and fostering a positive attitude towards yourself and quitting is the key to your success. It lies with you. You have the ability to make the changes you want to improve your life and your health and to feel really good about yourself. You hold the key to your own health and well-being – within yourself.

2. Harness the power of your mind to help create your perfect outcome, so your expectation – to stop smoking successfully – is in line with your success. Instead of setting out to quit and secretly worrying you'll fail, thinking 'I can't stop smoking' or 'it's too difficult', you can use your imagination – the greatest tool you possess – to turn this around and to reprogramme yourself.

3. Finally get rid of the fears and doubts (more about this in next session).

4. Know how to cultivate and maintain your success: determination, persistence and perseverance pay off.

5. Commit to furthering your goal every day to keep the momentum going and stay on track. This includes taking care of anything that is inconsistent with this goal.

The missing link

What else do you think you need? What was 'missing' in any previous quit attempts? Do you find that simply wanting to quit is usually not enough? You need to have a means of anchoring your desire to stop smoking in a very real and physical way – so it's not only a fantasy but goes all the way through you, like the writing in a stick of seaside rock candy. Go to your body and use visualization together with grounding to make your desire physical so that it goes all the way through you.

How do you deal with self-doubt?

You have the ability to bring about your success – and to sabotage it – consciously or unconsciously. So you also need to know how to deal with and dissolve any self-imposed obstacles. When you do the exercise that follows, you might find your fantasy of success contaminated by little thoughts of self-doubt creeping in – 'I'll never do it' or 'Here I go again'. Maybe it will be a physical feeling, like your stomach churning as you fantasize about your success, or maybe your mind's eye will show an image of some past failure. If this is the case, go to the 'Creating What You Want for Yourself' exercise on page 70.

Here's how grounding will help once you set it in motion:
• You will be able to manage the physical manifestations of your self-doubt – the critical 'voice' in your head, the churnings, the images.
• You'll notice these 'symptoms' more easily.
• You will find yourself increasing in certainty and confidence.
Finally, the technique also takes care of your fantasy by helping you bring it into reality – helping make it real. This is why it's important to do something at the end of the exercise, however small it may be, to make your fantasy real. Chuck out the ashtrays or talk on the phone without your usual cigarette. Make it 'concrete' and bring it into the present moment.

Risky situations

State which situations could be high risk for you, such as times when you experience anger, frustration or stress.

_____

_____

_____

_____

Use the following techniques to help you succeed in particular situations:

• Use the visualization technique, 'Creating What You Want for Yourself', to change your thought pattern. For example 'I'm really enjoying myself in so many other ways'.

• Observe yourself in high-risk situations when you reach for a cigarette.

• Continue using grounding as often as possible, especially when thinking about smoking.

• Continue to congratulate yourself on your progress.

SELF-COACHING TIPS

• _Experiments show that it generally takes around four weeks to create new habits. Do the visualization every day for a few minutes for four weeks and notice what happens._

• _Making changes doesn't have to be hard. Don't think of change as being 'difficult', see it instead as 'challenging'._

• _Keep your reasons for quitting in mind – these often boil down to the desire to be happier._

• _Advertising and other smokers often focus on how 'difficult' quitting is, but this is a myth. You just need to know how to stop easily, how to make stopping part of your everyday life and find what works for you._

• _Remember the power of your own mind and the words you choose. If you think or feel quitting will be difficult, it will be. If you think it'll be easy, it most likely will be._

• _People who are positive have far better outcomes than those who are negative and stressed._

• _Focus on what you want, not what you don't want: 'I want to smell gorgeous, fragrant, fresh' instead of 'I don't want to smell of cigarettes any more'._

• _Keep in mind your new identity and way of life so it's more attractive to you than the old one. You won't easily be able to change your habit if you continue to believe it gives you pleasure._

• Include positive images in your visualization and everyday life. See yourself as calm, relaxed, healthy and breathing freely. Imagine others seeing you this way! Practise turning down cigarettes, 'No thanks, I don't smoke'.
• Start associating 'pleasure' with other activities as a way of changing the patterns you've set up in your brain around smoking and pleasure.
• 'What we share intensifies', so share your success with others. Ask others for positive support.
• If you find you're struggling, get grounded, then check out with yourself how you're feeling. Keep repeating it until you know you're 'clear'.
• The more you practise, the easier things happen. Don't mope – celebrate!

Commitment scale

Now that you've mastered the visualization exercise 'Creating What You Want for Yourself', how confident would you need to be, on a scale of 1 to 10, to be ready to quit?
1 2 3 4 5 6 7 8 9 10
How confident are you that you are ready?
1 2 3 4 5 6 7 8 9 10

15 Session 3: Facing fears

'Be yourself more fully ... follow what beckons you', Thich Nhat Hanh, *The Path of Emancipation*

Welcome to this session, in which you continue to experiment with new ways of restoring calm to your life – and find out what works best for you. We often fear what's unknown. By facing our fears and making them known, we begin to diminish them. And weaken their power over us. We can take control of our feelings, rather than letting them have control over us.

What's involved in this session?

AIMS
• Identify and deal with any fears associated with quitting.
• Change activities that trigger your smoking by enabling you to observe yourself and behaviour from a calm, serene place.
• Stay on track.

WE WILL COVER
• Embarking on change.
• The essence of fear.
• Resisting change.
• Mastering fears.
• Health facts.

TECHNIQUE: CENTRING
SELF-COACHING TIPS
EXERCISES

'If you always come from a place of dissatisfaction, then you keep producing dissatisfaction', Ken and Elizabeth Mellor

FACING THE FEAR

Do you feel some fear when you think about quitting?

• Yes

• No

If you are, you need to:

• acknowledge the feeling;

• see the feeling as 'true' for you;

• accept it's OK;

• face it in order to 'digest' it, using grounding and/or centring.

'What we want prompts our knowing that we want it', Ken and Elizabeth Mellor

Getting closed down

Fears about stopping smoking are often associated with feeling deprived – that life will never be the same again; that you won't cope with the huge void created by the absence of cigarettes in your life. As a result, smokers become 'closed down', 'contracted' or 'withdrawn'. This is not natural for humans, whose systems thrive on being open and flowing, always seeking a place of balance and harmony. Being 'closed' is like swimming against the tide – it takes much more effort to do this.

REJOIN THE STREAM OF LIFE

Imagine you need to rejoin the stream of life but smoking is preventing you. How can you get your system to accommodate the pleasure, openness and ease that's available to you, without resorting to any 'enhancers'? If you were completely free of fears around quitting, what would you do?

_____

_____

_____

_____

Prove that at least part of you is already doing this.

_____

_____

_____

_____

If this is difficult, imagine you've already got what you want and you're living it right now.

RESISTING CHANGE

Embarking on change can be a big step. Strategies such as affirmations can definitely help, especially when you're well grounded. However, if you're experiencing resistance – even though you want to quit – it's important to ask yourself some questions.

What do I usually do when it comes to challenges?

_____

_____

_____

_____

What do I usually experience?

_____

_____

_____

_____

Is there a pattern? (For example, do I tend not to finish things?)
• Yes
• No
If 'Yes', what is the pattern?

_____

_____

Sometimes you can set up a whole cycle of despair. To break this pattern, you first need to be kind to yourself.

LOOK AFTER YOUR INNER CHILD

Imagine that you are a kind and loving parent to your vulnerable inner child. What would you say to that child?

_____

_____

_____

_____

How would you act?

_____

_____

_____

_____

At the same time as being kind to yourself, it's important to keep clarifying what you want, in terms of your smoking. This process is a bit like rinsing a bowl of uncooked rice under a tap – the water keeps getting clearer and clearer. Grounding can help with this.

Dealing with fear

A very practical and simple way to deal with fear is get into the habit of finding pleasure in other things. Quitters do all sorts of things:
- carry a piece of fur in a pocket to stroke;
- spritz themselves with a favourite perfume;
- snack on various healthy treats;
- stop and notice beauty all around;
- practise the centring exercise.

'Remember, what you focus on, is what you get. Energy flows to where your attention goes', Ken Mellor

Centring

The centring technique (see page 81) is especially good for quitters: our life force energizes and floods us – and this is depleted and diminished by smoking. So centring is a great way to restore vitality and happiness and experience a balance with others.

'When well-centred our systems flood with life; when not well-centred, the life force within us is diminished ... like turning down a dimmer switch on a light', Ken Mellor

When you're well-centred, you're aware of the withdrawal or temptation but not thrown by it; at the same time you're able to stay calm, peaceful and serene.
- It's particularly helpful in social settings, like the pub or a party,

where you might find yourself being tempted to smoke or take a stand about your smoking (or anything else).

• Use it whenever you feel intimidated, low on energy or disconnected.
• You can do it for a few seconds or much longer, but each time you do it, you're promoting the results you want.
• The more you do it, the more the natural drive of your system rushes to your aid and you stay centred for longer and longer.
• You can do it anywhere and the results are instantaneous.
• You'll experience feeling alive, fulfilled and a clear sense of self.

FEARS ALREADY MASTERED

Make a list of your achievements where fear was an issue. Just jot things down as they come to you, however silly they may seem now. Start as far back as you like.

1. _____
2. _____
3. _____
4. _____
5. _____
6. _____
7. _____
8. _____
9. _____
10. _____

Now rate your overall 'success' in terms of what you've already mastered where 1 is very poor and 10 is brilliant.
1 2 3 4 5 6 7 8 9 10

If your score is high, use it to boost your self-confidence, to help you quit and to move on. If your score is on the low side, keep repeating the exercises until your mastery – and your confidence – increases and you can let go of things in your system that are holding you back.

Knowledge is power

Most smokers are aware of health facts related to smoking. But it's important to have clear information on the damaging effects of smoking and what you're doing to your body. Look at the following 20 facts about smoking, then choose the five you find the most powerful or meaningful.

1. Lung cancer is the biggest cancer killer in the UK, causing over 120,000 deaths every year. That's a jumbo-jet's worth every single day, and more than the following combined: alcohol, cocaine, heroin, homicide, fires and car accidents.

2. Around 40,000 new cases of lung cancer are diagnosed annually – 90 per cent of them caused by cigarettes. Fifty per cent die within four months; only five per cent live for more than five years after diagnosis.

3. Cancers of the mouth, throat and oesophagus occur up to 10 times more frequently in smokers. Smoking is at the root of 30 per cent of all cancer deaths in the UK, including cancers of the stomach, bladder, kidney, colon and breast.

4. Smokers under 65 are twice as likely to die from coronary heart disease. Smoking also causes strokes and heart attacks, chronic inflammation of the respiratory tract leading to destruction of air sacs and chronic bronchitis and emphysema (which inflames the lungs, deteriorating them until breathing is impossible).

5. Smokers should expect to lose, on average, 10–15 years of life. That's five and a half minutes of your life for every cigarette smoked – the same amount of time it takes to smoke a cigarette.

6. One in four deaths amongst London men and one in eight London women are caused by smoking. The proportion of deaths from smoking is highest for people aged between 35 and 64 with an annual death toll exceeding 10,500.

7. Casual smokers are also susceptible to lung cancer, breast cancer and heart disease. Five cigarettes a day doubles your risk of breast cancer and heart attack, while 20 a day could increase your chances of breast cancer fivefold. You're eight times more likely to have a heart attack compared with a non-smoker.

8. Women who smoke during pregnancy risk complications in pregnancy and labour, abnormal foetal development, low birth-weight or sickly infants.

9. Women who smoke face increased risk of reproductive disorders, fertility problems and increased risk of miscarriage as well as cervical and breast cancer. Men who smoke face increased risk of impotence and fertility problems.

10. Toxic gases in cigarette smoke destroy the little hairs in the respiratory tract that guard against pollutants and infection. Smoke and pollutants are more easily able to penetrate your lungs; their accumulation increases your exposure to carcinogens and predisposes you to infection and bronchitis.

11. Passive smokers are at increased risk: lung cancer (24 per cent), heart disease (25 per cent), breast cancer (27 per cent).

12. Forty per cent of smokers do not collect their pension, compared to 14 per cent of non-smokers.

13. A ban on smoking in public places would save more lives (4,800) than are lost every year in road accidents in Britain (3,400).

14. The Trades Union Congress is calling for tobacco smoke to be classified as a 'hazardous chemical'.

15. Smokers are twice as likely as non-smokers to lose their sight in later life – smoking is linked to AMD (age-related macular degeneration), the leading cause of sight loss in the UK.

16. Cognitive decline in the elderly is an average of five times higher per year in current smokers than those who never smoked.

17. Nicotine wrinkles skin more quickly than exposure to the elements. Smoking breaks down collagen, so both faces and bottoms sag.

18. Cigarette smoke contains over 4,000 chemicals. As well as tar and nicotine, there is also carbon dioxide, ammonia and arsenic. At least 50 of these chemicals are known to cause cancers of the lung, throat, mouth, bladder and kidneys.

19. Smoking stains teeth, causes bad breath and increases the risk of oral and gum disease, as it constricts blood flow to gums. Most tooth loss in 19- to 40-year-olds is associated with smoking.

20. In 2004, five leading tobacco companies stood accused of a 50-year conspiracy to hide their knowledge of the damage smoking can cause. Damning documents at the heart of the tobacco industry were deliberately – and systematically – destroyed.

HOW DO YOU FEEL AFTER READING THIS LIST?

Were you aware of the extent of the damage smoking can cause?
• Yes
• No

Compare your health and life as a smoker with yours as a non-smoker.

_____

_____

_____

_____

Whose chances of a healthier, happier life do you prefer?
• Smoker
• Non-smoker
Now select one fact to remind yourself why you're quitting, or have quit.

_____

_____

_____

_____

> ### SELF-COACHING TIPS
> • *Notice what does work – not what doesn't.*
> • *Fears tend to exist in the here and now. Look at your fears as if they are in the past and ask 'What was I afraid of?'.*
> • *Shift your energy and attention away from 'striving' and 'struggling' to quit. This doesn't help. Instead, learn to accept what you're experiencing, affirm what you've accomplished and build on these by using the five toolkit techniques.*
> • *Learn to be open to loving yourself (smoking interferes with this); then you can be more open and loving to others.*
> • *If you want something, imagine you've already got it; just let go those thoughts, beliefs and structures that no longer serve you and allow yourself to be there.*

Commitment scale
What, if anything, do you need to help take you one step nearer to setting your quit date?

_____

_____

Rate your certainty of quitting successfully from 1 to 10:
1 2 3 4 5 6 7 8 9 10

16 Session 4: Resolving doubts

'Like the moon, come out from behind the clouds. Shine', Buddha

What's involved in this session?

AIM
- Identify and resolve any mixed feelings about quitting.
- 'Digest' obstacles instead of repressing them to release them from your system.
- Experience freedom and vitality.

WE WILL COVER
- Importance of dealing with ambivalence.
- Facing challenges around quitting.
- The 'X' factor.
- Staying connected.
- What smoking means to you.
- Use of language.
- Turning doubts into affirmations.
- Setting your quit date.

TECHNIQUE: UNIFYING
SELF-COACHING TIPS
EXERCISES

Well done for staying focused and committed in this way. I hope the steps you're mastering will be useful in other areas of your life too. This session is perhaps the most fundamental and pivotal one. It's the key to your freedom, helping you unlock or dissolve doubts or inner conflicts you might have about quitting. You can move on from the places where you're 'stuck' and 'unhook' or 'unsnag' yourself.

Are you motivated?

Consider the following facts:

• Most smokers want to quit – at least 70 per cent.

• 83 per cent wish they'd never started smoking.

• Between 20 and 30 per cent stop successfully (based on one year after quitting), using methods that include counselling plus NRT such as patches.

• However, around 70 per cent relapse (at one year) using NRT.

• Current research would have us believe that only around 3 per cent stop smoking successfully by going 'cold turkey', although there is a lack of evidence in this area.

So how come the success rate is so low? Unresolved mixed feelings...

TAKING RESPONSIBILITY

Take a few moments to get yourself grounded. Now ask yourself the following three key questions, making note of your physical responses.

1. Am I ready to take responsibility for my life and my health?

• Yes

• No

Describe your physical response.

_____

_____

_____

_____

2. Am I prepared to look at my lifestyle honestly and explore the issues necessary to make change possible?

• Yes

• No

Describe your physical response.

_____

_____

_____

_____

3. Am I willing to have faith in myself and my ability to cultivate a 'can-do' attitude and to commit to furthering my goal of quitting so I can achieve it easily and successfully?

- Yes
- No

Describe your physical response.

_____

_____

_____

_____

If the answer to all these questions is 'Yes', that's great. You're as ready as you'll ever be. If your answers include some doubts, these may reflect an inner conflict around quitting. Identify them here.

_____

_____

_____

_____

BOTH SIDES OF THE STORY

Do you want to stop smoking _but_ subconsciously believe it's the only way to enjoy yourself?

- Yes
- No

Do you want to stop smoking _but_ have an underlying and secret fear that life won't ever be the same again?

- Yes
- No

Do you want to stop smoking _but_ believe you need a cigarette to relax?

- Yes
- No

Do you want to stop smoking _but_ find yourself torn, even though you know it's harming you and those around you?

- Yes
- No

How do you account for your mixed feelings?

_____

_____

_____

_____

STUCK IN THE MIDDLE

The challenge for you is not so much how to unwind or enjoy yourself without cigarettes, it's about resolving a deep, inner conflict – where part of you wants to stop and part of you doesn't.

Would you agree this conflict feels like having your coat caught or snagged on a branch?

• Yes
• No

Would you like to be able to go back and unhook yourself, so you can walk away, free?

• Yes
• No

Does it also feel like having something caught in your system, an 'obstacle', you can't easily digest?

• Yes
• No

Do you believe, given the technique, you're able to resolve this problem, which has helped many smokers quit?

• Yes
• No

Are you willing to use your imagination and turn the situation around – so the 'obstacle' becomes something you embrace, instead of allowing it to hinder you, causing indigestion?

• Yes
• No

Are you also willing to allow it to nourish you before releasing it?

• Yes
• No

Do you still have mixed feelings about quitting?

• Yes
• No

Are you clear about what you want?

• Yes
• No

Do your feelings change from day to day?

• Yes
• No

The 'X' factor

What has kick-started your desire to quit? What has held you back for years, preventing you from quitting successfully?

_____

_____

_____

_____

All you have to do is resolve these two conflicting parts of you to help release your whole system from being 'stuck'. Then your energy can once again flow freely. You can stop smoking if you want to, and in a way that enables you to move on – freeing yourself from the dilemmas and fears that may have held you back.

Let's look at the 'two parts' – the one that wants to quit and the one that doesn't. First, it's important for quitters to recognize three major aspects when face to face with the real possibility of 'internal' change:
1. You need to identify and deal with your resistance to change, however slight you might think it is.
2. Motivation alone is often not enough.
3. You need to stay committed to furthering your goal by practising 'unifying' until you feel resolved.

STAYING CONNECTED

1. Do you use cigarettes as a way of avoiding staying connected to yourself?
• Yes
• No
2. Do you use cigarettes as a way of trying to stay connected to yourself?
• Yes
• No
3. Do you use cigarettes as a way of both avoiding staying connected to yourself *and* trying to stay connected to yourself?
• Yes
• No
4. If you answered 'Yes' to any of these questions, are you committed enough to yourself and your well-being to continue exploring and

experimenting with other ways of staying connected? This includes having faith in your own natural ability to deal with any mixed feelings, fears or other obstacles on the way?

• Yes
• No

If you answered 'No', it may be helpful to repeat the unifying exercise, described on page 89.

'We stay connected by staying aware of what we're experiencing', Ken and Elizabeth Mellor

What does stopping smoking mean to you?

As a smoking-cessation specialist advisor in inner-city Bristol, part of my job was to target areas of high health need – and this included pubs. It was great some punters were interested in quitting, but a few said things like 'What's the point? I might be run over by a bus next week'. Are you prepared to submit your health and life to an act of fate like being run over by a bus? Or have you decided to be in charge of your future and manage things differently?

_____

_____

_____

_____

Does your 'meaning' include caring about yourself and what happens to you?

• Yes
• No
• Don't know

If you answered 'Don't know', the unifying tool will help deal with these two aspects of you: 'I care about myself' and 'I don't care about myself'. Keep repeating the process until you feel resolved.

WATCH YOUR MOUTH

One way to start the process is to spot your doubts and, hence, your expectation of failure in your language. It also helps to notice other people's choice of words. Favourites include 'I might try and stop smoking next week' or 'I'm going to quit but a lot depends on my partner/work'.

What do you catch yourself saying or thinking about quitting that suggests your ambivalence?

_____

_____

_____

_____

How could you say it differently?

_____

_____

_____

How would you say it if your doubts were resolved?

_____

_____

_____

Make your dilemma conscious by practising unifying (see page 89 for a step-by-step description of the technique).

TURN DOUBTS INTO AFFIRMATIONS

Fear of change can be manifested in feelings of doubt and unwillingness to leave your comfort zones, old patterns and habits. It's important to be able to see your lifestyle and your future without cigarettes.

1. When you're excited, upset or anxious can you see yourself experiencing these feelings without having to have a cigarette?

• Yes
• Sometimes
• No

2. Would you like to experience finding your own stability inside yourself, instead of using cigarettes to do so?

• Yes

- Sometimes
- No

3. Would you like to experience change as the norm, rather than something unusual or scary?
- Yes
- Sometimes
- No

4. Are you willing to let go of old patterns of control, of using cigarettes as a way to deal with your feelings?
- Yes
- Sometimes
- No

5. Would you like to embrace life more fully?
- Yes
- Sometimes
- No

Now let's turn these questions into affirmations. Change 'you' to 'I', and turn each question into a statement in the present tense. The first one has been done for you.

1. When I'm excited, upset or anxious, I can see myself experiencing these feelings without having to have a cigarette.

2. _____
_____

3. _____
_____

4. _____
_____

5. _____
_____

Choose the statement you're most drawn to. Repeat it as often as you can – or keep writing it down.

How does your experience of unifying compare with the following statements?

When people have unified their conflicts, they generally experience much more ease and harmony and a feeling of relaxation and well-being.
- Agree
- Disagree

Unifying is a simple, powerful and effective way to resolve your feelings internally. It's a very effective way of setting yourself free – empowering and liberating you so that you can move on and achieve what you want much more easily.

- Agree
- Disagree

If you disagree with the statements, it may be that your experience feels more subtle, so persevere. Keep experimenting with unifying and give the technique some time. You'll find your awareness increases with practice, and you can experience the benefits regardless of how subtle your awareness may seem. The key is to really get into acting out each 'part' as fully as possible. Face and embrace every aspect, every thought, every feeling. Moving around helps increase these.

Decide to practise unifying regularly.

RESOLVING MIXED FEELINGS

Jot down which technique or techniques you could keep using to resolve any mixed feelings about why you smoke.

_____

_____

_____

_____

Knowing this may help you:

- be more aware of your addiction;
- be more alert to the patterns that trigger your smoking;
- start thinking about alternatives in difficult situations.

SETTING YOUR QUIT DATE

Now it's time to choose a date when you will stop smoking if you have not already done so. Decide which day of the week is the least pressured and which will allow you to change your routine (which contains your triggers), and make it a day when you can *treat yourself*.

If you don't feel ready at the moment, choose an imaginary quit date. Work towards it so that you're behaving as if you intend to quit then. Focus on that date and continue to master the techniques to help yourself be clearer and more confident. This will orientate you towards quitting.

Health Contract

I am living a completely healthy life.
I will never again have a cigarette.
I am free.

Signed

Date

Complete the above contract. Put a copy on the fridge or on the cover of your diary – to keep reminding you of your decision.

SELF-COACHING TIPS
• When you blame someone or something else for your failure to quit, you inadvertently 'empower' them (and your smoking) and disempower yourself.
• Feel good about what you're doing and never doubt it. If you find yourself experiencing doubts and mixed feelings, then keep repeating the unifying exercise until you feel clear.
• Always keep your eye on your goal, whatever the challenges.
• Experiment with flower essences. They are an effective, safe and natural way to help deal with fears and mixed feelings. They can ease anxiety, boost confidence and aid sleep as well as nourishing and enhancing spiritual, emotional and psychological well-being. Other quitters have reported good results.

Commitment scale

You are now clearer about your goal and how to achieve it.
How excited/delighted/pleased are you on a scale of 1 to 10 when you think about having set your quit date?
1 2 3 4 5 6 7 8 9 10

17 Session 5: Managing change

'If I'd known I was going to live this long I'd have taken better care of myself', Eubie Blake, American composer and pianist

Welcome to the final session. Stopping smoking is one of the very best ways you can take care of yourself. You may have quit already. I hope you're celebrating your great achievement and rewarding yourself. You deserve it. Rewards are a great way to keep reaffirming your success so keep on rewarding yourself. You can now enjoy maintaining your achievement until it becomes automatic behaviour, and you're living life much more enjoyably, to the full.

If you haven't quit yet, keep your momentum going by repeating sessions when you need to; this is also progress. You can set another quit date to help keep you focused, surer, clearer and more confident of your success. So stay with it. Perseverance pays.

What's involved in this session?

AIM
- The importance of reward.
- Train yourself to relax.
- Learn how to live your life differently.
- Enjoy the moment.
- Experience benefits of relaxation and other strategies.
- Understand the nature of stress and what to do about it.

WE WILL COVER
- Managing change.
- Nourishing yourself.
- Strategies for dealing with stress.
- Managing your weight.
- Rewarding yourself.

- Avoiding relapse.
- The five Ds.
- Building on your success.

TECHNIQUE: RELAXATION AND BREATHING EXERCISES
SELF-COACHING TIPS
EXERCISES

Managing change

Stopping smoking probably means a big change in your life, and change almost always involves a loss of structure. As a smoker, you tend to punctuate your day with cigarettes, which you associate with certain activities:
- tea breaks;
- after meals;
- when drinking alcohol;
- when dealing with stress.

The anticipation of losing this 'structure' often arouses fear and anxiety in smokers. To move through the change, we need to know how to manage our feelings about what's new and what's lost – even with changes that we want, or are enthusiastic about.

Nourishing the nervous system

Smokers use cigarettes to calm themselves, so quitters often crave nicotine when they are angry, frustrated or stressed. A good supply of magnesium is vital for relaxing muscles and calming the nervous system. Sources rich in magnesium, according to nutritional therapist, Nigel Hinchliffe, include:
- unrefined cereals;
- nuts and seeds;
- fruit and vegetables, especially dark green leafy vegetables like spinach, broccoli, kale, chard.

Take an additional 300 milligrammes of magnesium per day if you're experiencing withdrawal symptoms, such as agitation or irritability.

Serotonin levels in the brain can be reduced by withdrawal from nicotine. A milky drink in the evening will help increase levels and improve sleep or mood patterns. Compensate for lower serotonin levels by:
- eating foods like wholemeal bread and bananas;

- eating lots of fruit and vegetables (eight to ten portions a day), especially lemons, limes, celery and beetroot;
- cutting down on foods such as meat, dairy products and sugar;
- supplementing your diet with calcium, magnesium, and Vitamin C (consult a nutritionist for further advice);
- drinking lots of water, eight glasses a day, to help detoxify your body.

STRESS STRATEGIES

Do you usually feel stress about something that's just happened or is about to happen?
- Yes
- No

Do you usually feel stress in situations where you feel demands on you are high and control over decisions is low?
- Yes
- No

Is stress a key reason for lighting up?
- Yes
- No

Which strategies do you have in place to help you deal with stress when you're no longer relying on cigarettes?
- Grounding (connecting you with your body and the outside world);
- Centring (adopting a 'non-attached' attitude whereby you 'observe' yourself from a place that's calm, peaceful, serene);
- Unifying (resolving conflicts and doubts);
- Creating What You Want for Yourself;
- Relaxation/breathing exercises (rejuvenating, restoring);
- Physical activities such as yoga or tai chi (for reducing stress/adrenaline levels);
- Meditation;
- Other

_____

_____

Which situations do you think you might need to use them?

_____

_____

Write down one thing that indicates a step forward when it comes to taking care of yourself.

_____

_____

The joys of relaxation

Relaxation is a great natural way to restore health and vitality and help you feel at peace with yourself – whether or not you've quit yet. You'll find there are so many benefits:

• You'll manage pressure better without feeling you have to rely on anything.

• Your relationships will improve. You'll find you're able to be closer, more intimate and more loving with others (instead of relying on your 'little friends').

• Living in the present moment means you can let go of worrying thoughts, be calmer and more easily able to stand back from things.

• You'll be better able to focus, concentrate, and you'll deal with problems more easily.

Taking up yoga or meditation as a way of relaxing can help instil a sense of peace and joy; it can lead to greater fulfilment and happiness and permeate your whole being. Even five minutes a day makes a difference. It's also a great way to continue maintaining your commitment to yourself.

SELF-COACHING TIPS

• *The quickest way to reduce stress and bring down adrenaline levels is to focus on your breathing.*

• *If your desire to smoke is strong, say to yourself 'I don't have to stop smoking. But if I want to feel well, I need to quit. I am responsible.'*

• *Use the techniques to reconnect with your 'true' self in a way that's calm and clear and can bring a sense of freedom, ease and vitality within you – and with everything around you.*

Manage your weight

Most quitters tend to gain, on average, 4 pounds (1.8 kilograms). You might feel hungrier than you're used to, because smoking acts as an appetite suppressant. Putting on weight could set up a negative cycle, where you relapse because you've gained weight. So avoid this pitfall – and continue taking one step at a time. Exercise regularly to manage your weight while you are quitting.

It's not a good idea to diet whilst quitting. Focus on one thing at a time. When you know what to eat, you're less likely to gain weight.

SELF-COACHING TIPS
1. Be clear about what you want. Be specific about your ideal weight (this could change later): 'I want to weigh 10 stone/65 kilograms'.
2. Go for what you want, not for what you don't want. Remember to phrase it in the present tense. Say 'I am my ideal weight of 10 stone', instead of 'I don't want to be overweight'.
3. Only settle for the very best – the 'go for gold' picture.
4. Use 'I am' affirmations and picture and feel the truth of your goal 'internally'.
5. Practise grounding at the same time – this is important to help digest your experience, where you imagine every cell in your body is celebrating with you.
6. When finished, behave as if it were true by doing something in line with your visualization – for example, eating a piece of fruit or drinking a glass of water. See the water as life-giving.
Practise the exercise daily, or as often as possible and, like quitting, take care to behave in a way that maximizes your chances of success: watch what you eat and exercise regularly.

Curb cravings

Did you know you can curb cravings by eating certain foods? The right nutrition can provide the support your body needs to reduce cravings, manage weight and promote optimal health. According to Nigel Hinchliffe, nutrition can help with cravings and withdrawal symptoms by balancing blood sugar levels (BSLs).

Nicotine cravings are often due to a drop in BSLs, causing irritability, loss of concentration and a dip in energy. Avoid the temptation to give yourself a sugar boost.

• Eat a good breakfast (eggs, muesli, porridge, fresh fruit with nuts and natural yoghurt).

• Choose high-fibre foods such as vegetables, fruits and grains. These

may also help regulate the bowel (smoking and bowel action are often associated).
• Top up your protein levels: eat fish, eggs, meat, nuts and seeds. (Lentils and beans provide both fibre and protein.)
• Plan your snacks and treats so you've got them to hand. A small tub of hummus and oatcakes makes a delicious snack – or try apples, nuts or dried fruit.
• Treat yourself so you associate quitting with pleasure, not deprivation.
• Avoid sugary food and refined flour like white bread, biscuits, cakes, chocolate and sweets, as these directly affect your BSLs.
• Take a supplement to help reduce cravings and to stabilize BSLs, such as Biocare Sucroguard, which contains B vitamins, magnesium and chromium.

Reward yourself

It's important to keep rewarding yourself to reaffirm your success – with yourself and others. What are you going to do with all the money you save? List some ways in which you're rewarding your success, determination and good health. For example, treating yourself to a relaxing treatment or buying flowers or a meal for a supportive friend.

_____

_____

The danger of relapse

Quitters say relapse is due mainly to:
• Old patterns that crop up, such as using cigarettes as a way of repeatedly comforting yourself when you're under pressure or feeling 'low'.
• Spending endless amounts of mental energy on quitting, as well as negative 'self-monitoring' resulting in low self-esteem.
• Being unprepared for 'triggers' such as stress, alcohol or socializing – the 'Sod it, I'll just have one' factor.
You may be feeling discouraged or feeling a failure. Remember the following rules:
• Acknowledge and encourage your strengths.
• Be a friend to yourself rather than an enemy.
• Nurture yourself.
• Be confident of your success.

Remember

- Keep repeating techniques for staying calm and grounded.
- Think of yourself – and see yourself – as a non-smoker, not a smoker.
- Decide you're worth it.

The five Ds

1. **Delay:** cravings only last a couple of minutes.
2. **Deep breathing**: to help you relax (the oxygen will increase alertness).
3. **Decide** to think positively. See the experience as an important opportunity for learning about yourself. You are taking care and control of your life without the need of cigarettes.
4. **Drink** water – it helps cleanse the body of toxins. Eight glasses a day is the recommended minimum.
5. **Do** something else: keep yourself busy.

Take one day at a time and congratulate yourself on each day of your success. (Source: advisors' manual, 'Support to Stop' Avon NHS)

TAKE YOUR CONCERNS IN HAND

Make a list of your 'challenges' and your concerns.

1. _____
2. _____
3. _____
4. _____
5. _____

What action are you taking?

_____

_____

Are you willing to see the situation as one in which you're training yourself to be the master of your own destiny?

- Yes
- No

Enjoying your success

If you have not yet quit at this stage, you have lots in common with someone who has.

- You have worked hard to achieve your goal.

- You have recognized and dealt with obstacles.
- You have changed your mindset on smoking.
- You have persevered.
- You have stayed committed.

Three things are vital:

1. Congratulate yourself. Acknowledge your great achievement. Your success. Your freedom.
2. Remind yourself why you quit.
3. Prepare yourself. This is important. See page 104, where you list any triggers or old patterns along with which techniques you will use for dealing with them. For example:

- An argument: grounding/breathing;
- A drink: centring;
- A problem: 'Creating What You Want for Yourself' (to experience things working out for you).

Maybe you've already quit – or maybe you've been here before. That's fine. We learn by repetition, by taking ourselves back over and over the same ground – until we get it right. So see any previous attempts as a measure of how serious you are about wanting to quit.

Time to reflect

You now know how to cultivate and maintain your success for as long as you need, until your confidence is automatic. You possess a proven set of techniques to help sustain you over the coming weeks. It's important to keep relating to your goal as being permanent, whether or not you've quit, so that should any triggers occur that might tempt you into old patterns, you will know you are capable of turning things around. You now have other options, other choices about how you respond to certain situations, so you don't need to continue to behave in a way you don't want. Instead, you can be in charge of your life and your health.

I hope you decide to make quitting a top priority and continue building on your success so far. Be kind to yourself, and patient. Take care of yourself and enjoy taking responsibility for achieving your goal. Help yourself become clear about what you want and, if necessary, repeat the sessions until you feel fully grounded in your new-found freedom, reconnected to your true self and everything around you. I wish you every success and a long and healthy life.

Resources and information

For stop-smoking coaching, further information and training in the techniques mentioned in this book, see www.stopsmokingcoach.net.

The techniques made available in the toolkit are adaptations based on the teachings of Ken and Elizabeth Mellor, which are available as audio tapes and CDs through Biame Network (www.biamenetwork.net) and all good bookshops. The CDs contain relaxation exercises to recharge or revitalise you, or to help you get to sleep. Meditation exercises are: Grounding Meditation, Creative Release Meditation (Creating What You Want For Yourself), Centring Meditation, Unifying Meditation and Relaxation Meditation.

Sources of further information

Action on Smoking and Health (ASH), www.ash.org.uk

Treatobacco.net (Database and Educational Resource for Treatment of Tobacco Dependence), www.treatobacco.net

No Smoking Day, www.nosmokingday.org.uk

British Heart Foundation, www.bhf.org.uk

British Lung Foundation, www.britishlungfoundation.co.uk

National Asthma Campaign, www.asthma.org.uk

Cancer Research UK, www.imperialcancer.co.uk

Index